W9-BSS-080

Savion Glover

ENTERTAINER

Black Americans of Achievement

LEGACY EDITION

Muhammad Ali

Maya Angelou

Josephine Baker

Johnnie Cochran

Frederick Douglass

W.E.B. Du Bois

Marcus Garvey

Savion Glover

Alex Haley

Jimi Hendrix

Langston Hughes

Jesse Jackson

Scott Joplin

Coretta Scott King

Martin Luther King, Jr.

Malcolm X

Bob Marley

Thurgood Marshall

Jesse Owens

Rosa Parks

Colin Powell

Chris Rock

Sojourner Truth

Harriet Tubman

Nat Turner

Booker T. Washington

Oprah Winfrey

Black Americans of Achievement

LEGACY EDITION

Savion Glover

ENTERTAINER

Judy L. Hasday

CHELSEA HOUSE
PUBLISHERS
An imprint of Infobase Publishing

Savion Glover

Copyright © 2006 by Infobase Publishing

Chelsea House
An imprint of Infobase Publishing
132 West 31st Street
New York NY 10001

Library of Congress Cataloging-in-Publication Data

Hasday, Judy L., 1957-
  Savion Glover / Judy L. Hasday.
      p. cm. — (Black Americans of achievement, legacy edition)
  Includes bibliographical references and index.
  ISBN 0-7910-9223-2 (hardcover)
  1. Glover, Savion—Juvenile literature. 2. Dancers—United States—Biography—Juvenile literature. 3. Choreographers—United States—Biography—Juvenile literature. 4. Tap dancing—United States—History—Juvenile literature. I. Title. II. Series.
  GV1785.G56H37 2006
  792.7'8—dc22   2006011038

Chelsea House books are available at special discounts when purchased in bulk quantities for businesses, associations, institutions, or sales promotions. Please call our Special Sales Department in New York at (212) 967-8800 or (800) 322-8755.

You can find Chelsea House on the World Wide Web at
http://www.chelseahouse.com

Series and cover design by Keith Trego, Takeshi Takahashi

Printed in the United States of America

Bang FOF 10 9 8 7 6 5 4 3 2 1

This book is printed on acid-free paper.

All links and Web addresses were checked and verified to be correct at the time of publication. Because of the dynamic nature of the Web, some addresses and links may have changed since publication and may no longer be valid.

Contents

The Colors of Classical Savion

To see Savion Glover perform live, with all his energy seemingly channeled right down through him to his feet, is to truly experience his genius talent as a dancer. The stage is rather plain, almost by design. There are no distractions as Glover's feet dazzle and astonish an audience watching him do what he does better than anyone: Tap!

There is a slight riser-type platform, perhaps 10 feet by 6 feet, front and center stage. Classical musicians, all dressed in black, accompany Glover for this night's performance. They include Eugenia Choi, Robert Norman, Shih-Hung Young, and Melissa Tong on violin; Jessica Meyer and Tom Rosenthal on viola; Rafal Jezierski and Clara Lee on cello; and Kevin Mayner on bass. All are seated higher behind the "tap" stage. Later, an infusion of jazz will be added by the members of The Otherz: Tommy James on piano, Andy McCloud on double bass, Patience Higgins on saxophone and flute, and

Brian Grice on percussion. Without much fanfare, the lights dim, Glover is introduced, and out he walks onto the stage. If you have never seen a Glover performance live, or read about what he "does," the setting and rather simple start of the show might seem rather mundane. But once the first note is struck, and the first tap sound "clicks," the simplicity becomes anything but mundane.

THE COLOR ORANGE

This night, the only tidy part of Glover is his signature dreadlocks. Looped together up on the back of his head rather than falling loose, his braids do not swing around unless the sheer power of kinetic gravitational pull releases them from their elastic band. Glover's rather basic attire, composed of black slacks and a tank top-style white undershirt, is offset by the only vivid color on stage—the orange of his open, billowing, button-down shirt, which he is wearing slightly draped off his muscular shoulders. The unbuttoned sleeve cuffs and shirt give the appearance of a performer who was caught when he was not quite put together, but who nevertheless had to go onstage. In reality, during the two-hour show (with no intermission), the informality of the dress is necessary for Glover to perform. Instead of looking unkempt, the shirt, which becomes darker from blotched patterns of sweat as he dances, is just part of the fluid motion that is Classical Savion.

In *Classical Savion*, Glover's latest choreographed one-man dance show, eighteenth-century composers Johann Sebastian Bach and Wolfgang Amadeus Mozart have replaced the blues, and 'da noise and 'da funk are offered up in rhythm to the sounds of composers like Antonio Vivaldi and Béla Bartók. As Julinda Lewis wrote in "Classically Offbeat Savion Glover" for the *Richmond Times-Dispatch*, "For some, it might be disturbing to have tap dance accompanying Vivaldi's *The Four Seasons*, or to add tap percussion to Mozart's Divertimento in D Major or Dvořák's *American* Quartet. And was Bach's

With a small orchestra in the background, Savion Glover dances during a dress rehearsal of his show *Classical Savion* at the Joyce Theater in Manhattan. In the show, Glover tapped to music by the likes of Vivaldi, Mozart, Bach, Bartók, and Mendelssohn. His tap shoes were like another musical instrument in the orchestra.

Brandenburg Concerto No. 3 ever intended to be conducted by some peripatetic man in tap shoes?"

As Glover begins to move his feet to the sounds of *The Four Seasons*, starting with the third movement of "Summer," he seems to be conducting his musical ensemble with his feet, rather than a baton. On his "tap" platform, Glover uses all of the available space, moving forward and backward, side to side, covering every inch of his surface, constantly moving his feet, either subtly or with a force so pronounced that the "tap" sounds like a metallic drum. In actuality, Glover is not doing conventional tap, though the steps and kicks and hits are definitely tap moves. But instead of the sounds that come off his size-12½ Capezios complementing the music, the sounds from Glover's shoes are like another musical instrument. They seem to play notes written in a musical score for the instrument "tap shoes," just as there would be notes for the violins, violas, cellos, and bass. Only this instrument is loud and animated, attached to a lanky, bearded "maestro of movement," as Glover is described by *Providence Journal* writer Bryan Rourke. "Glover is not just a dancer, but a composer and musician, a percussionist whose instrument is his feet, with which he plays a remarkable array of rhythms and complex orchestrations," Rourke wrote.

Just like an orchestra conductor, Glover seems completely focused on his musicians and the music. He appears to know the music intimately, note for note, as if he studied it in depth before scoring the part for himself. During the remainder of *The Four Seasons* ("Autumn" and "Winter"), Glover is in complete sync with the pace of the music. Again, in keeping with the absence of any color besides his shirt, four tall, black speakers have been strategically placed in each corner of the tap platform. Instead of facing out toward the audience, they are turned inward as if to allow Glover to hear and analyze the interplay of the music and his incredible footwork.

CAPEZIOS AS A MUSICAL INSTRUMENT

As is the case with most musical instruments, where the musician has a choice of manufacturer (for example, Steinway, Yamaha, and Baldwin all make pianos), so, too, does the "tapper." Some musicians prefer the tonal sound quality of a Steinway to a Yamaha, or the smooth melodic sound of a Stradivarius to a Guarneri violin. So, too, does a tapper have choices in tap shoes.

Because tap dancing creates sounds as well as movement through space, the instruments (the shoes) used to create those sounds are very important. Tappers have choices in shoes and taps. A performer can choose street shoes (possibly with an additional overlaid sole) or specialty dance shoes, and a range of metal taps that can be used with each. To have the screws attach the taps adequately, a thin fiberboard spacer is often used in combination with leather soles. The spacer is glued and tacked down. Unwanted rubber heels are replaced by stacked leather heels made by a cobbler. The "toe box," the shoe area around the toes, can be constructed in a range from light to heavy. A heavy toe box would assist in structural support for specialty moves like toe stands. A "high box" would allow for more toe freedom within the shoe. There are also fiber or metal shanks that add stiffness along the length of the shoe. Balance between heel and toe is also important. The range of shoes can run from a light jazz tap shoe with taps over a suede sole and a minimal toe box, to a sturdy two-tone "Spectator" shoe with double sole, reinforced toe box, and support shank.

Glover slips his size-12½ EE feet into Capezio Tap Oxfords. Salvatore Capezio, a master cobbler, opened his shop in New York City in 1887 at Broadway and 39th Street, just across from the old Metropolitan Opera House. The sixteen-year-old Capezio hung a simple sign above his door that read "The Theatrical & Historical Shoemaker." Glover's taps of choice are the three-screw mounted Capezio Tele Tone toe and heel taps.

When Glover dances, he seems totally into the music and how his feet contribute to the overall sound. In his autobiography, Glover has a diagram of his musical instrument—his tap shoe sole. Glover explains how he hears the percussion sounds and creates them in *Savion: My Life in Tap:*

> I know my feet, all about them. It's like my feet are the drums, and my shoes are the sticks. So if I'm hearing a bass sound in my head, where is that bass? Well, I have different tones. My left heel is stronger, for some reason, than my right; it's my bass drum. My right heel is like the floor tom-tom. I can get a snare out of my right toe, a whip sound, not putting it down on

the floor hard, but kind of whipping the floor with it. I get the sounds of a tom-tom from the balls of my feet. The hi-hat is a sneaky one. I do it with a slight toe lift, either foot, so like a drummer, I can slip it in there anytime. And if I want cymbals, crash crash, that's landing flat, both feet, full strength on the floor, full weight on both feet. That's the cymbals. So I've got a whole drum set down there. And knowing where all those sounds are, knowing where I'm trying to get them from, that's how I go about creating the step.

As the tempo of the music changes, so too does the speed of Glover's feet. Claudia La Rocco of the Associated Press wrote after a *Classical Savion* performance, "Whether filling in the spaces between the notes with his nuanced, staccato rhythms, punctuating crescendos or hammering away against the melody, Glover's feet managed a rare feat, simultaneously reimagining the music and allowing its vibrant essence to come to the fore." At one point during the first movement in the "Autumn" section of *The Four Seasons*, Glover finally reveals the object he has been holding in his hand since he first came onstage. What looked like a mini baton is a screwdriver, which he uses to adjust a screw in the toe tap. Though it is not always necessary to tighten tap screws during a performance, brisk tapping can vibrate the screws loose. The way Glover taps, it is a wonder the screws do not fly off the soles of his Capezios.

THE COLOR BLUE

With the tempo of Vivaldi's composition picking up speed, Glover's feet follow. Though his steps, crossovers, jumps, and slides look entirely improvised, each step has been carefully choreographed to each musical note in keeping with the orchestral arrangement for the accompanying instruments. By the time the third movement of "Autumn" is over, Glover's orange shirt is more dampened by his sweat than dry, and he makes a momentary exit offstage. When he returns, he is wearing a fresh, dry shirt, this one a steel-blue button-down shirt. The orchestra begins playing Allegro non molto, the first movement of Vivaldi's "Winter." The quick-paced violin solo over the softer, single-stroked note played by the other stringed instruments sets Glover in motion, and his feet no longer look as if they are attached to his ankles. They move and bend from side to side, then upward and over, rolling almost in a 360-degree motion. Loud thwacks are replaced by a subtle sound of "tickety bloo kah."

Moving and tapping his way through other classical pieces by Mozart (accompanied beautifully by flutist Patience Higgins of The Otherz), Dvořák, Bach, Bartók, Shostakovich, and Mendelssohn, Glover amazes the audience with his soft steps and sudden change into explosive rat-a-tat-tat staccato steps, jumps, splits, and leaps off the stage. His body is constant motion. Glover often appears as if he is about to lose his balance—then he recovers quickly. Though he rarely makes eye contact with the audience, he often does with the orchestra. Most of the time, his back is to the audience, but when he turns to face them, he is often wearing a childlike, innocent grin, as if to convey the sheer joy he is experiencing. His body posture is rarely upright; his upper body is usually somewhat hunched over, as if exhausted. His right hand (with screwdriver tightly gripped) seems to be moving, as if rapping a drumstick. The fingers on his left hand look as if he is just barely snapping them in rhythm to the music. Sometimes, Glover even appears to be dancing with his shadow.

EVERY INCH OF THOSE 12½ EEs

No matter what musical piece is being played, Glover's feet keep moving. Sometimes he taps one foot while the other is in midair. Sometimes he rolls one foot as if he is skating across the stage. Even when he seems to be just walking, you hear the soft tap, tap, tap on the stage. There are moments when Glover looks like a boxer, dancing in training. The raw power of his athleticism momentarily takes over his slender but powerfully conditioned body. Every inch of his Capezios are used: in one moment Glover slides back his right leg and raps a tap-tap-tap riff off the tip of the shoe in unison with the violins. Then he leans over and thwacks down the other leg as if in a horse gallop. United Press International writer Frederick M. Winship describes how the musical arrangements "allow Glover to demonstrate his most evocative tap techniques, including insistent tattoos of foot beats, subtle chatter of patterned sound that imitates singing along with the music, and various forms of percussive stamping, sliding, gliding, and shuffling."

His blue shirt soaked in sweat, Glover exits offstage to change into a dry shirt for his finale, which shifts the sights and sounds from classical to jazz with "The Stars and Stripes Forever (for Now)," an interpretation of composer John Philip Sousa's march. While Glover is changing, The Otherz bass player Andy McCloud comes onstage and warms up the crowd to the purity of jazz, plucking the notes on his double bass strings as they could respond to his fingers alone. The music takes the audience back to a time of smoke-filled jazz clubs. The classical musicians behind McCloud offer soft accompaniment to his riffs, lulling the audience into a calm before the storm of Glover's return.

THE COLOR RED

Back onstage, Glover is wearing a bright red shirt, already showing Rorschach-like blot patterns of sweat, even though he has just put it on. Before sending the audience into kinetic delirium with "The Stars and Stripes Forever (for Now)," "this sinuous jazz symphony serves initially for the dancer to introduce each musician onstage, allowing for some virtuoso solo work," *Daily Variety* said. "As the classical and jazz

A portrait of Gregory Hines and a pair of Savion Glover's tap shoes were perched atop a piano during a dress rehearsal of *Classical Savion* in January 2005. Glover dedicated the finale, "Stars and Stripes Forever (for Now)" to his mentor, Hines, who died in 2003 of liver cancer.

players riff off each other with playful verve, the piece evolves and assumes darker tones—echoed in Brenda Gray's stylish lighting design—while Glover hammers out a brooding, ambiguous interpretation of war and power that gives new punishment to the wooden platform…" What follows the interlude with the musicians is breathtaking and exhausting to watch. Glover seemed to save his best for last, moving his entire body at a locomotive pace, keeping in step with every note of the marching-band style of music. He seems to dance endlessly, once again soaked in sweat, but now smiling more broadly, as if to show the audience the sheer pleasure he feels at moving fast and free.

Classical Savion ends as it began, with little fanfare. Glover takes a few solo bows and then has the ensemble join him in a group bow. The lights on the stage go dark, and Glover simply walk-taps off. The concept of *Classical Savion* was a collaborative effort between Glover and producer-arranger Robert Sadin. Both were looking for music with "an edgy subtleness." Glover explained, "The show we have come up with is about this solo dancer needing this music. Needing to challenge this music, you know? How dare there not be a tap dancer around when this music is being played?" After seeing Glover perform, how dare there not be a tap dancer around, indeed.

2

Stealing Steps

The *Off Jazz Dance World* Website defines tap dancing as a "style of American theatrical dance, distinguished by percussive footwork, that marks out precise rhythmic patterns on the floor. Some descriptive step names are brush, flap, shuffle, ball change, and cramp roll." Because of the dynamic, rhythmic sound that is unique to the dance form, tapping identifies the performer as not only a dancer but also as a percussive musician. Though tap is an American art form, many of its elements, like most things "American," have their origins outside of our geographic borders.

A MIXTURE OF STYLES

Tap was evolving long before artists like Fred Astaire, Sammy Davis, Jr., and Gregory Hines were demonstrating their step combinations in the metal tap-plated shoes that are the standard of today's tap footwear. This evolution started "when

West African musical culture, based on drumming and rhythm, was brought to this hemisphere with the slaves," according to *Savion: My Life in Tap.* Glover wrote:

> It spread through the Caribbean, mixed with the syncopations of the islands, and then came to this country. Immigrants from Ireland and France and England and Holland had already settled here with their own traditions. What resulted was a cross-fertilization of European and African cultures. As people shared with each other—and borrowed and stole—new kinds of songs emerged. New beats. New rhythms. New dances.

Today's tap dance is a mixture of many ancestral dance styles, including the English clog, the Irish step dance, and African "juba" and "ring shouts," boisterous dances with a recurring beat. Watching tap dancing, you can also see the familiar frenzied movements made popular in swing dance and the Lindy Hop, or the gentle rolling glides recognizable in the steps of the waltz and the fox trot. What would become American tap dancing emerged during the early days of vaudeville, which was a variety show that presented comedy acts, singing, dancing, mimes, and even animal acts. Three styles of tap dances were seen in vaudeville—kicking dances like the Charleston, the buck-and-wing fast dance style using wooden-soled shoes made famous in minstrel shows, and the soft-shoe, which created a lighter tap sound from semi-stiff leather-soled shoes on a hardwood stage. Writer Genevieve Thiers, in her article "The History of Tap Dancing," explains what happens when these all came together: "When these three styles mingled, tap dance became a dance with a beat governed by noise, with a leather shoe and metal sole."

TAP PROGRESSES

There is no doubt that tap dancing evolved as music evolved. The PBS series *The Blues* describes the music that tap emerged with:

The passionate and uniquely American art form known as the blues was born in the steamy fields, dusty street corners and ramshackle juke joints of the Deep South in the late 1800s. An evolution of West African music brought to the United States by slaves, the blues emerged as Southern blacks expressed the hardships, heartbreak, religion, passion, and politics of their experiences through a blend of work songs, field hollers, and spirituals.

As travel became easier and the demand for labor in the cities of the northern United States increased with the industrialization boom, many black Americans packed up their belongings and left Southern cities like New Orleans, Louisiana, and Jackson, Mississippi, for places like Kansas City, Chicago, and Detroit. As the migration moved north, regional influences had an impact on the blues sound, eventually evolving into ragtime, swing, and jazz.

The tap dance trendsetters congregated at dance clubs like the Hoofers Club in Harlem, the section of New York City that was the creative center in literature, art, music, and dance during the height of the Harlem Renaissance in the 1920s. At places like the Hoofers Club, tap aficionados would hone their skills and square off in tap challenges, or "cutting sessions." Challenges were a form of one-upmanship, where one dancer tried to outdo the other dancers. It was also during these basement or back room contests that an unwritten law emerged—one understood by every tapper, that copying someone else's exact steps was forbidden.

Stealing steps and challenges have long been a part of tap's colorful history. Stealing steps referred to a dancer's trying to figure out what another dancer was doing and how that dancer was getting a particular sound from his or her steps. What resulted was a slight modification of the step, creating yet another challenging movement or improvement in tap dance that also fit that dancer's personal style. In a reference to stealing steps in their book *Jazz Dance: The Story of American Vernacular Dance*, Marshall and Jean Stearns write about one such occurrence by tap great John Bubbles:

> Bubbles, however, had little trouble adopting other dancers' steps. He had a reputation of being cagey, and his technique for extracting a step from a competitor became notorious. Watching another dancer practicing at the Hoofers Club, Bubbles bides his time until he sees something he can use. "Oh-oh," he says, shaking his head in alarm, "you lost the beat back there—now try that step again." The dancer starts only to be stopped, again and again, until Bubbles, having learned it, announces, "You know, that reminds me of a step I used to do," and proceeds to demonstrate two or three variations on the original step. The other dancer usually feels flattered.

BUCK WING, SHUFFLE, AND SLIDE

An audience's view of tap dancing as entertaining was not always seen in the most positive light. In the early days of tap, vaudeville and minstrel dancers who appeared onstage in blackface—white performers who painted their faces with black makeup—would mimic black field hands in their dance routines. Within these tap dance numbers, Genevieve Thiers wrote, there were "certain movements of the feet ... originally meant to indicate clumsiness, buffoonery, and running away"—derisive suggestions of the days of slavery.

There were many black dancers, however, who made the art of tap dancing anything but irreverent or slavery-mocking. Many blacks took on the joy of tap dancing as a means of creative expression. William Henry Lane (also known as Juba), a free black man from Rhode Island, learned to dance from saloon hall dancer "Uncle" Jim Lowe. Lane was dancing the jig and incorporating shuffle and slide steps into his routines around the 1840s. He was also the first to add syncopation and improvisation. In his book *Black Dance in America*, James Haskins writes that Lane placed an "emphasis on rhythm and

Salvatore Capezio

The creator of the signature dance shoe that bears his name, Salvatore Capezio was born on April 13, 1871, in Muro Lucano, Italy. His father was a construction engineer, but the younger Capezio was not interested in going into his father's trade. Instead in 1887 at age 16, he opened his own business at Broadway and 39th Street in New York City, across from the famous old Metropolitan Opera House. The sign he hung above the door read "The Theatrical & Historical Shoemaker," thus founding a company that became known for stocking specialized dance apparel and the repair of theatrical shoes including ballet pointe shoes. Though he started out mostly repairing shoes for the Metropolitan Opera, a chance emergency request to make a pair of shoes for opera tenor Jean De Reszke led to Capezio's transition from repairing shoes to creating them.

In crafting shoes, particularly ballet pointe shoes, Capezio discovered that there was a fine balance between the shoes' delicate design and their complex engineering. Soon, Capezio's reputation as a master shoemaker traveled through the dance and theater world. His shop was often a gathering place for dancers, who stopped by to discuss their shoe needs and entrusted Capezio to meet them. As the business grew, Capezio imparted his shoemaking design secrets to members of his family who joined the company. In no time, Capezio-crafted shoes were on the feet of dancers in the *Ziegfeld Follies* and other major Broadway shows. When fashion designer Claire McCardell displayed her Capezio-made long-sole ballet shoes with her latest clothing collection in 1941, high-end stores like Lord & Taylor and Neiman Marcus began to buy and promote Capezio footwear. Today, Capezio is one of the largest and most respected makers and suppliers of footwear and dance apparel in the world, providing ballet, tap, and ballroom dance shoes, as well as ice skates.

Included among Capezio's most famous clients are Russian ballerina Anna Pavlova, who bought Capezio pointe shoes for herself and her entire company while on tour in the United States in 1910; tap legends Honi Coles and Gregory Hines; and dancer-entertainers Gene Kelly, Fred Astaire, and Sammy Davis, Jr. Recipient of the Coty Award in 1952, the fashion industry's highest honor, Capezio continues to recognize excellence and achievement in dance by awarding The Capezio Dance Award.

Dancer John Bubbles is shown in his 1935 role as Sportin'
Life in the George Gershwin opera *Porgy and Bess*. Bubbles
is acclaimed as the "father of rhythm tap."

percussion rather than melody." Lane toured the northeastern
part of the United States to take part in challenges, and he was
even known to tour with white dancers when performing his
solo act, not an easy accomplishment for black dancers in the
early days of tap's emergence. Lane must have been quite a
tapper, because his legacy lives on even though he died in 1852
at age 27.

There were other great tap masters who appeared on the dance scene in the early part of the twentieth century. King Rastus Brown perfected the buck dance—a blend of a shuffle and tap move, dancing flat-footed. Born in 1902, John William Sublett, whose stage name was John Bubbles, is hailed as "the father of rhythm tap." While still a youngster, Bubbles teamed up with Ford Lee Washington in a song-and-dance act billed as Buck and Bubbles. Bubbles sang and danced while Buck played the piano. Bubbles developed a more sophisticated dance act soon after his voice changed, cultivating "a new style of tapping that blended extremely difficult innovations such as double over-the-tops (a rough figure-eight pattern done with a deliberate near tripping technique)," according to the *African-American Registry* Website. "Bubbles would do them while alternating legs, traveling backwards and forwards, and from side to side. By 1922, Buck and Bubbles reached the top in vaudeville by playing at New York's Palace Theatre." On his own, Bubbles, who came from Louisville, Kentucky, was chosen in 1935 to create the role of Sportin' Life in George Gershwin's opera *Porgy and Bess.*

PEG LEG AND THE NICHOLAS BROTHERS

Many other great black tap artists emerged during the height of the dance style's popularity. Clayton "Peg Leg" Bates, who

IN HIS OWN WORDS...

When asked during an interview what he would do if he broke a leg or had some other injury that would not allow him to dance, Savion Glover looked bewildered and said:

Ever heard of Peg Leg Bates? I would tap with my elbows, anything ... anything with music.

loved to dance, lost his left leg in an accident when he was 12 years old. Despite incredible obstacles, Bates taught himself how to dance using two broomsticks until his uncle fashioned him a peg leg. In a short period of time, Bates was dancing as if he had two good legs. Peg Leg began dancing at carnivals and county fairs and was soon discovered in 1927 at the Greenville Black Liberty Theatre in South Carolina by a New York City producer. By this time, he had mastered the ability to jump five feet in the air and was able to perform almost every tap dance step known to man. "He performed at the Lafayette Theatre in New York with Bill 'Bojangles' Robinson. In a brief time Bates was a showstopper, dancing at the Apollo Theater, the Cotton Club, and resorts and clubs throughout the United States," according to the entry on Bates at *South Carolina African American History Online.* "He gave two command performances before the king and queen of England." Bates was truly a remarkable inspiration to anyone with a physical disability, demonstrating that a handicap need not prevent people from doing what they love.

Long before Gregory Hines and his older brother Maurice were taking their show to the stage, the Nicholas Brothers— Fayard and Harold Nicholas—had been hailed as the greatest and most beloved tap dance team in entertainment history. Sons of musicians, the Nicholas brothers grew up in Philadelphia, Pennsylvania, under the watchful eye of their parents, who played in their own band at the old Standard Theater on South Street. Having spent so much time at the theater, the boys were exposed to most of the black vaudeville acts of the times, including the dance acts, and they were soon inadvertently putting their own act together as they clowned around and imitated what they had seen. Soon they were the talk of the entertainment circuit and found themselves performing at places like the Lafayette in New York City.

From their successful run at the Lafayette, the Nicholas Brothers wound up being featured at the famed Cotton

The Nicholas Brothers, Fayard (left) and Harold, show off some of their moves in the 1943 film *Stormy Weather*. The brothers appeared at the famed Cotton Club in Harlem and went on to perform for nine presidents of the United States.

Club in Harlem, where they performed for two years with the likes of musical greats Cab Calloway and Duke Ellington. During their six-decade career, Fayard and Harold appeared in several Hollywood films, danced as part of the *Ziegfeld Follies* on Broadway, and toured internationally, performing for the king of England, U.S. troops in Vietnam, and nine presidents of the United States. Recipients of numerous awards, the Nicholas Brothers received a star on the Hollywood Walk of Fame in 1994. Harold died in 2000 at the age of 79; Fayard passed away in January 2006 at age 91.

BOJANGLES AND BEYOND

Perhaps the most well-known black tap dancer of all was Bill "Bojangles" Robinson. Born in Richmond, Virginia, on May 25, 1878, Robinson began dancing for a living at age six. He toured with Mayme Remington's troupe and then joined the company of *The South Before the War* when he was 12. As an adult, under the careful management of Marty Forkins, Robinson gained publicity and prominence by working solo dance gigs in nightclubs. When Lew Leslie, a white impresario, produced *Blackbirds of 1928*, a black revue for white audiences, Robinson was hired as a feature performer. He later became a top vaudeville star and finally a Hollywood motion picture star. He appeared in 17 films, including *The Little Colonel* (1935), *In Old Kentucky* (1935), *The Littlest Rebel* (1935), *Rebecca of Sunnybrook Farm* (1938), and *Just Around the Corner* (1938). Robinson also appeared in what he called his favorite film, *Stormy Weather*, an all-black musical released in 1943.

Of Robinson's unique personal tap style, Marshall and Jean Stearns wrote, "He brought it up on the toes, dancing upright and swinging....The flat-footed wizardry of King Rastus Brown, although some old-timers still prefer it, seemed earthbound compared to the tasty steps of Bojangles, who danced with a hitherto-unknown lightness and presence." Robinson's soft-shoe steps and tap routines were probably copied by other dancers more than anyone else's. He was probably unsurpassed in his ability to create new steps, the most renowned being the Stair Dance. He also had the uncanny ability to run backward, setting a record of 8.2 seconds in the 75-yard dash. Though a generous and bighearted man, Robinson died penniless in 1949. About his dancing versatility, Robinson once said that his feet responded directly to the music—his head had no part in it.

There were many other tap greats who did not receive the same recognition as their white counterparts, such as

Tap dancer Bill "Bojangles" Robinson was a leading vaude-ville star who later appeared in 17 motion pictures, includ-ing several with child actress Shirley Temple. Here he is seen with Lena Horne in his favorite film, *Stormy Weather*, which was released in 1943.

Fred Astaire, Gene Kelly, and Donald O'Connor, did—people like Charles "Honi" Coles, Ralph Brown, Charles "Chuck" Green, Bunny Briggs, Lon Chaney, and Jimmy Slyde. It was not until tap sensation Gregory Hines appeared on the scene and started working with these men that their names began to be synonymous with tap dance. And then came Savion Glover, their child protégé who took tap dancing by storm as a young seven-year-old in search of teachers, of the unknown masters of the art. When Savion was born in 1973, Honi Coles, Jimmy Slyde, Bunny Briggs, Chuck Green, and the rest could not have imagined what an impact this young boy from Newark, New Jersey, would have on the art that is tap. It was Savion's phenomenal success and following that allowed him to bring recognition to these men—recognition long overdue, and richly deserved.

3

Tapping in the Womb

Destined to be "special," dance sensation Savion Glover was born on November 19, 1973, in the northeastern New Jersey city of Newark. Glover's mother, Yvette, had not picked out a name for her son ahead of his birth, but she believed in her heart all during her pregnancy that this unborn child was going to be someone extraordinary, she says, because she was told so by God. "He gave me the name," Yvette Glover said in *Savion: My Life in Tap.* "I'm not a fanatic, but I am religious, and when I was in the hospital, I said, 'God, I don't have a name for this baby.' And I closed my eyes, and the slate of a blackboard, as black as it can be, appeared before me, and He wrote the name out in script—He didn't print it; it was in script: *Savior.* And I said, 'Now, you know I can't name him Savior.' So I took out the *r* and put in the *n.*"

Though Yvette had been wed at 18, the marriage did not last. She never married again. Savion is the youngest of Yvette

Glover's three children. She has two other sons, Carlton and Abron, and all three boys have a different father. Unlucky in love, Yvette ended up disappointed in one way or another by the fathers of her sons. Each time she became involved with one of these men, she thought that this relationship was the one that would last. In retrospect, Yvette just chalks up the lost loves to hopes and foolish dreams on her part. Yvette, like her sons, was the product of a broken home and a family that struggled financially. She was one of six children of Wilbert and Anna Lundy Lewis. The family lived cramped together in a one-and-a-half-room house at 452 Washington Street, not far from the roar and traffic of Newark International Airport, as well as within eyeshot of the hustle and bustle of the theater mecca of the United States: New York City.

MUSIC IN THE GENES

Savion's family tree is showered with musically gifted relatives. His grandmother Anna was a gospel singer and played the organ. Grandfather Wilbert was a singer and a keyboard player who was often away on musical gigs in the Catskill Mountains in upstate New York. The resort area was nicknamed the "Borscht Belt" for its mostly Jewish-owned bungalow colonies, summer camps, and small hotels. The Catskill resorts provided thousands of jobs for college students who sought work over the summer to help finance their educations. Of equal importance, the Borscht Belt provided many aspiring singers, musicians, and comedians access to a stage to hone their talents while entertaining vacationing audiences. "For decades, predominantly Jewish crowds flocked to the green mountains and grand hotels of the Catskill Mountains north of New York City for fresh air and caustic jokes, big bands, and mountains of all-you-can-eat food: rib steaks, blintzes and borscht (hence the nickname, the Borscht Belt)," Brian Knowlton wrote in an article in the *International Herald Tribune*. Describing the atmosphere, former dance instructor Jack Homer said in the same article: "It was like New Year's Eve every night. We danced all day and danced all night, then we danced some more."

When Wilbert wasn't on the road, he and Anna often sang as a duo in the nightclubs around Newark and New York City. Yvette Glover also remembers musicians piling into their small house to jam. "When her mother shooed Yvette and her little sisters and brothers upstairs to the landlady's apartment, to get them out from underfoot, the children listened to quartets through the floor," Robert Johnson wrote in *The Star-Ledger* of Newark. Yvette showed some of her own musical talent—she liked to sing, so her mother put her in the church choir. The church offered a comfortable place to relax and socialize with other church members. In Johnson's article, Yvette Glover said:

> My mother was an extraordinarily gifted and brilliant woman. Wherever she went to play, I was right there. So I started going to church. And at that time, my friends and I, we stayed in church all day. We had so much fun! We would run up to the nearest restaurant, and see who could get there first to hold the seats, then go back and sing in the choir. That's when music was music, and that's all we could do.

Today, Yvette Glover is a gospel and jazz singer, having put off her own musical career for years while she raised her sons and worked as Savion's manager, traveling companion, and spiritual advisor as he carved out his own career. But do not call her a stage mother. Yvette often responds to such comments by saying that she never gave birth to a "stage!" "I'm a late bloomer," she said, taking inspiration from the late Alberta Hunter, who after a 20-year hiatus returned to her career as a blues singer at age 82. Yvette has performed in America and Europe, and one Internet biography lists her as becoming one of the most in-demand jazz vocalists in the United States. Just as her parents before her did, it is not unusual for Yvette to show up spontaneously at a local jazz bar, like Ashford and Simpson's Sugar Bar, on 72nd Street between West End Avenue and Broadway in Manhattan, or The Crossroads, a local restaurant-bar in Garwood, New Jersey. Every Tuesday night at The Crossroads is "Open Jazz Jam" and performers are welcome to play and sing along with the in-house trio. But her success today seemed just a faint dream as she struggled early in her adult life to raise three boys alone in Newark, New Jersey.

NEWARK'S BEGINNINGS

The city of Newark, New Jersey, has a long history marked by periods of growth, decay, and renewal. Founded in 1666 by Puritans who had earlier settled in Connecticut, Newark is the third-oldest major city (Boston and New York are the first two) in the United States. Newark is actually the city's second name. It was originally called Milford, after the Connecticut town from which many of its settlers came. The Newark of today so little resembles the town settled 340 years ago, it is hard to imagine it was founded by the Puritans of New England. "So stern was the government of the Newark church-state that not to belong to the church meant one was actually outside the law and not subject to protection or benefits of Newark's township form of government," according to the city of Newark's Website. "It was not until Colonel Josiah Ogden dared to harvest his wheat on a Sunday that Calvinism met its first challenge, and oligarchic government was ended."

During the colonial era (1600–1775) in America, Newark was a city known for its industry and commerce, including its beer, cider, and tanned leather products. The city grew rapidly around its manufacture of leather. Massachusetts transplant Seth Boyden, who came to the city in 1815, developed a process for creating patent leather, which contributed to Newark's becoming the nation's largest producer of leather by 1870. In that year alone, the industry brought $8.6 million in revenues into the city. Also contributing to the city's industrial growth was the 1831 construction of the Morris Canal, which linked Newark to the surrounding major iron and farming areas of the state. The arrival of the railroad helped boost the already flourishing shipping business, and Newark developed into one of the most important industrial centers in the northeastern United States. The banking and insurance industries contributed to Newark's commercial rise. Both Mutual Benefit (1845) and Prudential (1873) were founded in Newark and today remain among the nation's leaders in their industry.

PEAKS, VALLEYS, AND HARDSHIP

Newark's early commercial and industrial success, however, would not last. According to Newark's Website, the city in the twentieth century was:

> … marked by boom and bust, peaks and valleys, hardship and hope. In 1916, nearly everybody took time to reflect in a yearlong celebration of Newark's founding. But a peaceful atmosphere was tested by national and international crises, two world wars, the worst depression in the nation's history, the Korean and Vietnam conflicts, and the terrible national riots in 1967. While the factories churned out products of war on a 24-hour basis, people were displaced and families uprooted.

In time housing projects went up, the city budget fell despite a tax increase, and many middle-class and upper-middle-class residents moved out of Newark, settling into the rolling hills and open farm country nearby and creating

This photograph from 1916 shows the bustling business district around Broad and Market streets in Newark, New Jersey. That year, the city held a yearlong celebration of its founding. The economic success of those times, though, did not remain consistent during the twentieth century, and the city was in bad shape when Savion Glover was born in 1973.

affluent suburbs. Transportation improvements, including the construction of the New Jersey Turnpike, Interstate 280, and Interstate 78, hurt the floundering city as well in two ways—by tearing down the infrastructure of the neighborhoods they went through, and by providing highways that gave workers the ability to commute to and from Newark while living outside the city.

Newark began a racial transition in 1940, when blacks from the South began migrating to the North to find jobs. From 1940 to 1970, 5 million blacks made their new homes in the cities up north. And though Newark saw a drop in its overall population (from 438,000 to 408,000) from 1950 to 1960, it took in 65,000 non-whites in that 10-year period. By 1966, Newark had a black majority, one of the fastest change-overs in racial composition of America's Northern cities. The tragedy and irony of the Great Migration was that as more and more poor Southern blacks were moving north to try to secure jobs in the industrial sector of Newark, the jobs were evaporating.

THE NEWARK RENAISSANCE

The development of the "New" Newark Movement, which began in the 1950s, helped to slow Newark's downward spiral. Commercial giants Prudential and Mutual Benefit made the commitment to rebuild their corporate headquarters in the troubled city. Other companies soon followed their lead in helping to revitalize Newark. Mayor Leo P. Carlin led the government's contribution by overseeing job-creation projects, including the expansion of the city's airport and Port Newark seaport. Rutgers University and Seton Hall University expanded their presence in Newark as well.

Still, the continued existence of poor housing, discrimination, crime, and job loss might have been too much to overcome had it not been for the guidance of Kenneth Gibson, who in 1970 was the first black man to be elected mayor of a large northeastern city. Gibson forged a second "New" Newark Movement, and since then, many positive changes have occurred. City historian Charles Cummings explained:

> Two decades ago, applying the term "Renaissance" to Newark might have seemed unrealistic, but today it seems appropriate. The great new downtown

Gateway towers are stunning examples of the state's largest office complex....The new PSE&G tower is being closed in by the march of new buildings up Raymond Boulevard. Newark Center incorporates both Seton Hall Law School and a commercial structure, and One Penn Center adds a stunning southern anchor to the complex....Small business establishments are refacing their facades. Newark Airport has become one of the nation's busiest and most important international air centers. A $375 million monorail now links the terminals to the parking lots (plans are proposed to link the monorail with the downtown areas of both Elizabeth and Newark). The universities and colleges are expanding and bringing national recognition to the community, and the newly refurbished Newark Museum is proving to be a major cultural asset.

In 1997, the New Jersey Performing Arts Center opened its doors, bringing about 1.6 million people into the city who might not have visited otherwise. They took in headline shows by such diverse entertainers as Itzhak Perlman, 'N Sync, and the Alvin Ailey American Dance Theater. Sports enthusiasts can sit in the stands of Riverfront Stadium to watch the minor league baseball games of the Newark Bears. In keeping with the commitment to be a part of Newark's revitalization, the New Jersey Devils of the National Hockey League will get a new arena, which is slated for completion in 2007.

MAKING ALL THE SACRIFICES

Though Newark is aiming to recapture the prosperous days of its early modern development, it was not the ideal place to raise a family when Yvette Glover was trying to do the best by her sons, Carlton, Abron, and Savion. Brenda Mitchell, a friend of Yvette's for more than 50 years, recalled those hard times: "She made all kinds of sacrifices. There were times when she wouldn't buy clothes for herself at all, but her children were impeccable. She took them everywhere with her and tried to expose them to life, and she set a very good example for them." Yvette worked various jobs, from sewing men's ties in a factory to assembling children's toys. She worked for a dry cleaner and, after studying business, took jobs as a secretary at Newark City Hall and in the state's Office of Administrative Law. At times, even that was not enough, so Yvette moonlighted as a waitress to earn extra cash.

There were even rougher times in the Glover household—mother Anna and sister Arlene and her son moved into the tiny apartment Yvette shared with her boys. When times were dire, Yvette had no choice but to go on welfare. Still, she was determined to make the best life she could for her family and herself. She struggled to give Carlton, Abron, and Savion all the opportunities she could, all the while looking to the future. Somehow she managed to send the boys to parochial schools. Robert Johnson wrote in *The Star-Ledger*:

> A week's vacation for them all, at her church's summer camp in Pennsylvania, was a necessity, even if it meant returning to find the Rose Terrace apartment padlocked because the rent was late. She gathered the boys around her on the porch to look at the stars, and strove to keep the atmosphere in their home loving and cheerful.

The boys grew up in a happy, loving home, shielded from the harsh realities of their day-to-day struggles. "Out of the worst situations came laughter," Savion recalled. "If our lights were off for some strange reason, we lit candles and sang songs."

RESPONDING TO RHYTHM

Savion's father, Willie Mitchell, did not have musical skill, but he could dance, according to Yvette. A carpenter by trade, Mitchell had the movement and physique to dance well—a trait that attracted Yvette to him. Between her parents' musical talents, her own, and Mitchell's fantastic rhythm, the components were all there for a musically gifted child. "While still in the womb, this baby responded to rhythm," according to the *Star-Ledger* article. "Glover's co-workers at the Office of Administrative Law touched her belly to confirm that the child's movements followed the carriage return on his mother's typewriter."

Even as a baby, Savion astonished his family with his musical acumen. "Shortly after Savion's birth, his grandmother Anna Lewis ... held the crying infant to her shoulder and began to hum a soothing refrain. To her great surprise, the baby hummed the tune back to her. She almost dropped him," the *Star-Ledger* article continued. Before he learned to crawl, he was already grabbing things and banging them together to make his own rhythm—all prior to his first birthday. Often, Yvette would come home to find that Savion had dragged out pots and pans and lids from under the sink, which he would just start banging. "He'd just have to be making sounds. He would beat up on the wall, he'd beat on anything. He'd beat on me or you if you were there," Yvette said.

When Savion began to walk, he did not walk with his feet flat on the ground. Instead, he would lift himself up onto his tip-toes, walking around almost on pointe like a *danseur noble* (male ballet dancer). It was not unusual for Yvette to come home some evenings and find a miniature theatrical production awaiting her, performed by Carlton, Abron, and Savion. Finally, when Savion was four and a half years old, Yvette enrolled all three boys in Suzuki classes at the Newark School of Performing Arts. The Suzuki method, a technique for learning to play musical instruments developed by

Shin'ichi Suzuki, by then in his 80s, is shown teaching violin to a class of children in Great Britain. Suzuki believed that learning was connected to repetition, and youngsters around the globe have learned to play musical instruments based on his philosophy. When Savion Glover was four and a half years old, his mother enrolled him in a Suzuki class.

Japanese violinist Shin'ichi Suzuki, is based on the observation that young children learn to speak a language by imitating others. The child learns to look, listen, and imitate the actions necessary to play.

MUSICAL PRODIGY

It wasn't long before Savion placed out of the Suzuki classes and moved into regular music classes with older children. Because he was so gifted musically, he was given a scholarship. At the school, Savion received his first real musical training and learned how to *really* play the drums. Before long, his talents were introduced to the world outside his classes or living room. One winter day in 1980, Yvette brought her six-year-old son along to a rehearsal of her gospel group. The group was meeting at the home of her manager Rudy Stevenson, a jazz musician who plays guitar, flute, and banjo. He has also

Shin'ichi Suzuki

Shin'ichi Suzuki was born on October 17, 1898, in Nagoya, Japan. He was one of 12 children, all of whom played near their father's violin factory. Though Suzuki often observed how this lovely instrument was made, it was not until he was a teenager that he realized what beautiful sounds came from playing it. He was astonished when he heard a recording of Schubert's *Ave Maria* being performed by legendary Ukrainian-born violinist Mischa Elman.

Enchanted by the musical instrument's sound, Suzuki brought a violin home from the factory and taught himself how to play. He did so by listening to a musical recording and trying to reproduce what he heard. When he was 22, Suzuki traveled to Germany to study violin with Karl Klinger. During the eight years that he lived in Germany, Suzuki was under the guardianship of famed scientist Albert Einstein. Suzuki also met his wife, Waltraud, while in Germany. The two married and moved back to Japan, where Suzuki began to teach violin and perform in string quartet concerts.

Suzuki had a special love for children and developed a strong interest in teaching them. He believed children could learn music in the same way they learned to speak their language: "He discovered that through rote learning children as young as three can reproduce on an instrument what they have heard played." Suzuki believed that there was no such thing as talent; rather, the secret to successful learning was directly linked to repetition. Over time Suzuki and many of his students traveled to play in countries around the world. More and more teachers became interested in Suzuki's "Talent Education" philosophy, and they began implementing the Suzuki method in their own musical classes. Today, thousands of children around the globe who play instruments learned to do so through the Suzuki method. Suzuki's method of learning, though, was never his primary goal: "Teaching music is not my main purpose," he wrote. "I want to make good citizens, notable human beings."

been a studio musician for performers like Nina Simone and The Fifth Dimension. During a break in rehearsal, Stevenson heard the rhythmic sounds of drums being played somewhere in the house. When he went to investigate, he found Savion pounding away on the skins. Stevenson had three young sons of his own who were also rather accomplished musicians— one was a bass player, another played saxophone, trumpet, and flute, and one son about Savion's age played the piano.

Stevenson put Savion together with his sons to hear them play. In no time, the quartet, which was known as Three Plus, started playing in public. In his autobiography, *Savion: My Life in Tap*, Glover recalled:

> I stopped taking drum lessons when I got into the band. Three Plus. I was the plus. Me and Rudy Stevenson's kids. We were good, man. We did standards like "Take the A Train," "In a Sentimental Mood," but we could also kick it. We'd have the people rockin', man. We played schools, outside festivals. We'd just set up on the street and do performances. Basically we would perform anywhere.

IN HIS OWN WORDS...

In *Savion: My Life in Tap*, Savion Glover remembers that day when he was at the Broadway Dance Center and saw Lon Chaney and Chuck Green perform:

> I was maybe seven years old, and all up to this time I had never thought of dancing. It never crossed my mind, even though I was hip to it. I was hip to Fred Astaire-type dancing, his kind of smooth dancing, and I dug it, but I'd never seen rhythm dancing before. It wasn't until that day that I'd ever seen Chaney and Chuck do their thing. And I watched them and I was like, Wow! That had different rhythms going than I had ever heard before. And it was with their feet! They were just really laying down all the rhythms. And I was totally fascinated.

Three Plus was doing well and getting known around the local band circuit. After two years of performing in parks and at parties, Stevenson got Three Plus a benefit gig at the Broadway Dance Center (renamed in 1984 from the Hines-Hatchett jazz and dance studio), a well-known dance school in Midtown Manhattan. There, Savion first saw legendary tappers Lon Chaney and Chuck Green. Savion was blown away by the rhythms coming from their shoes. His enthusiasm did not go unnoticed by his mother. In *Savion: My Life in Tap*, Yvette recalled that day: "I remember I was sitting there, and during intermission ... Frank Hatchett announced they were taking enrollment for dance school. And I said to myself, 'Now look, if Savion's got this much rhythm, then sign him up for dance.' And that's what I did." Savion Glover's career in dance was about to begin.

4

The Tap Dance Kid

When Yvette Glover enrolled Carlton, Abron, and Savion into dance school, she probably was not thinking that her decision might set career paths in motion for her sons. She had not even known about the conversation Savion had with Lon Chaney the day he was playing drums with Three Plus at the Broadway Dance Center. Savion recalled the conversation, "And I remember I followed Chaney into the dressing room, this big bear kind of a man with a low, rumbly voice and he told me he had been a drummer before he was a dancer. And he was like, 'You were doing some good rhythms on the drums,' and I was just a little kid, so I didn't say anything. And he said, 'You should try to dance.'"

As with everything else musical, Savion entirely took to tap dancing. His particular passion was for rhythm tap, a type of tapping that uses all the areas of the foot to create a sound. Rhythm tap is also known as "hoofin'" or "buck tap" and is the type of tap dance in which the foot is used as a musical instrument. Savion wasn't particularly well-outfitted for his entrée into tap class. Without enough money available to buy tap shoes, Savion went to class in three-quarter-length, beige Thom McAn cowboy boots. The boots had a hard sole, hard enough to get the "tap" sound. Savion was never fussy about where he practiced his tap steps—at home, on the sidewalks outside his house, on store floors while shopping with his mother. Anywhere he could move his feet and get a sound, that was where Savion tapped.

When he was finally able to put aside his cowboy boots for some real tap shoes (his first pair were red and white), Savion really started to focus more on speed. "When we got tap shoes, then it was like, Wow, this is what it's about. And I started thinking about speed, being fast," he wrote in *My Life in Tap*. "As a matter of fact, I used to think it was all about being fast. Diggitydiggitydiggitydiggity again and again, always about speed, diggitydiggitydiggitydiggity." In an interview with Jae-Ha Kim for the *Chicago Sun-Times*, Savion confessed that he was probably a nightmare for his neighbors because he tapped everywhere. The one consolation, Savion thought, was that his feet were much smaller as a preteen, so perhaps the thunderous "bang" of him landing on his taps wasn't quite as shattering to the peaceful silence that his "thwacks" disrupted.

IN HIS OWN WORDS...

As a child, Savion Glover was never at a loss for a place to dance. As he said in *Savion: My Life in Tap*:

> I would dance when I was walking. I would dance when I was waiting for the bus. I would dance on the bed, dance in the shower. I'd just dance. I was just happy to be dancin'.

HONING HIS TAPPING SKILLS

Savion was quickly turning heads with his incredible dance skills. Aside from taking his lessons at the Broadway Dance Center, he was soon performing at tap festivals with the true masters of the dance form, including Lon Chaney, Jimmy Slyde, Chuck Green, Honi Coles, and Bunny Briggs, to name a few. The men showed Savion the real style of "hittin'" the floor with all areas of the foot, to acquire that particular percussive sound that is tap.

Savion was never far from Yvette's sight. She would accompany him to his classes and then find a quiet out-of-the-way spot to sit and work on her crossword puzzles (Yvette loved doing crosswords) or read her Bible. She kept far away from the din of the other "dance" moms, who were talking away about their kids or recipes they just had to try. One day in 1983 while Savion was "hittin' the wood" in class, the producers of the Broadway musical *The Tap Dance Kid* came to the center to create a workshop for young tappers. They wanted to establish a stable of talented dancers for the show.

A year later, before Savion had reached his eleventh birthday, he was asked to audition for the show. In his interview with Yvette for the *Star-Ledger*, Robert Johnson wrote about the audition:

> Then one day, as Glover was enjoying her crossword puzzle, waiting for Savion to emerge from class at the Broadway Dance Center, a voice called to her. Unexpectedly, she was whisked into the studio, where choreographer Danny Daniels had come to audition her son for the title role in *The Tap Dance Kid*, the part that would catapult him to fame.

BROADWAY BOUND

Savion's singing and dancing did not bowl over the staff of *The Tap Dance Kid*, but his dance talents were so over-the-top that everyone connected with the show—the producers, the casting agent, and the choreographers—had the same reaction. They all realized they were in the presence of a young man who was, if not a dance genius, then certainly close to it. Yet, even with Savion just on the cusp of breaking into the big time, Yvette wanted to make sure that he would not be sacrificing his childhood. Yvette did the unthinkable—she resisted signing the initial contract for *The Tap Dance Kid* because it required Savion to give up sports activities. Yvette had just bought a new bicycle for her son, and she knew that he loved to strap on his roller skates and glide around the neighborhood, as well as play basketball and football with Carlton and Abron.

To say that Norman Rothstein, the show's general manager, was stunned by Yvette's stance would be an understatement. He told Yvette that in all his years in the business, he had never had a parent tell him no to such an opportunity. According to writer Robert Johnson, Yvette told Rothstein, "I'm not taking Savion away from being a boy. Thank you very much." Ultimately, everything was worked out. Yvette and her sons also consulted their pastor, Delbert Baker of the Newark Bible Fellowship Church, for guidance. The church had always been the Glovers' foundation. They were firmly grounded in their spirituality, which would always play an important role in their lives.

Soon, the news spread in the Glovers' Newark neighborhood that Savion was going to perform on Broadway. Yvette even remembers the kind words from people on the Green No. 56 bus, which she had ridden for so many years. They had gotten to know her so well over time that if she was late getting to the bus because of sending the boys off to school, they would insist that the driver wait for her. Said Yvette, "When Savion got his first break, they knew what had happened. It was all in the paper. They said, 'Girl, if anyone deserves this, you do.' They cried. They applauded. They were so happy for me. It was unbelievable."

Tap dancing legend Charles "Honi" Coles appears at a benefit in 1990 at Lincoln Center in New York City. After Savion Glover began taking lessons at the Broadway Dance Center, he had the opportunity to perform at tap festivals with masters like Coles, Jimmy Slyde, and Bunny Briggs.

A BOY BORN TO DANCE

The Tap Dance Kid opened on Broadway at the Broadhurst Theatre on December 21, 1983. The musical was based on a novel titled *Nobody's Family Is Going to Change*. Published in 1974, the book was written by Louise Fitzhugh, an award-winning children's novelist. The original cast starred New York native Alfonso Ribeiro, who is known for his role as Carlton Banks, the cousin of Will Smith's character in *The Fresh Prince of Bel-Air*; stage and television actress Hattie Winston; and Hinton Battle, who won a Tony Award for his portrayal of Dipsey in the show.

The show centers on the life of a 10-year-old boy named Willie Sheridan. His father, William, is a successful lawyer, and his mother, Ginnie, now a homemaker, was once a stage performer. Older sister Emma wants to follow in her father's footsteps and become a lawyer. Contrary to his father's wishes, Willie only dreams about becoming a professional show dancer. Instead of toy trucks and sports gear strewn about his room, Willie has posters of dance greats Fred Astaire and Bill "Bojangles" Robinson adorning his walls.

Whenever Uncle Dipsey comes to visit his niece and nephew at their home on Roosevelt Island in New York City, Willie and Emma plead with him to tell stories about the days when he, Ginnie, and Daddy Bates (Dipsey and Ginnie's father) used to perform as a trio. William, though, is more interested in grades and scholastic excellence than in having his children's heads filled with stories about the theater. This sets the stage for Willie's struggle—going against his father's wishes and attaining his own aspirations. Perhaps one of the most enchanting moments in the musical comes when Willie auditions for Dipsey's show. So caught up in the moment, Willie falls into a Technicolor fantasy in which all of his dancing idols—Fred Astaire, Bill "Bojangles" Robinson, Gene Kelly, the Nicholas Brothers, even Dipsey and Daddy

Louise Fitzhugh

Children's author Louise Fitzhugh was born in the grand Southern city of Memphis, Tennessee, on October 5, 1928. The only child of lawyer Millsaps Fitzhugh and Louise Perkins, baby Louise was raised by her father. Shortly after Louise's birth, Millsaps filed for divorce from his wife and won sole custody of his daughter, leaving young Louise to grow up without ever knowing her mother. Louise lived a mostly lonely childhood, which would be reflected in her writing as an adult.

Fitzhugh went to Miss Hutchison's School for Girls, an exclusive college preparatory school, and attended three colleges without ever obtaining a degree. She took some time to travel around Europe before returning to the United States and settling in New York City to engage in a career as a painter. In the late 1950s, Fitzhugh dabbled in her first publishing venture, providing the illustrations for friend Sandra Scoppettone's 1961 children's book *Suzuki Beane*.

In 1964, Fitzhugh published her first novel, *Harriet the Spy*, the story of 11-year-old Harriet M. Walsh, a wannabe writer who decides that she must be a spy, eavesdropping on others' conversations to learn all she could. Writing in the *Village Voice Literary Supplement* in 1995, Karen Cook describes the similarities between Fitzhugh and her fictional character: "Fitzhugh's alter ego is a mixture of bravado and candor, loneliness and humor, impulsiveness and an insistent delight in such routines as her daily tomato sandwich. No matter how tattered her relations with the world or her family may become, Harriet survives on her inner life, her artistic desire." Fitzhugh wrote a second book in the series, *The Long Secret*, published in 1965. It would be nine more years before her next novel, *Nobody's Family Is Going to Change*, would be published. The story explored the status of women's rights and children's rights and became the basis for the Broadway show *The Tap Dance Kid*. Though the protagonist in Fitzhugh's novel was a strong-willed 11-year-old girl named Emma, the theatrical adaptation centered on Willie, her brother.

Fitzhugh died suddenly in 1974 at the age of 46 from a brain aneurysm. Fitzhugh's executor Lois Morehead generated new material from what was left behind, culminating in the release of three books for young children, *I Am Five*, (which came out in 1978), and *I Am Three* and *I Am Four* (which came out in 1982). Fitzhugh's signature novel, *Harriet the Spy*, was made into a feature-length film in 1996.

Savion Glover made his Broadway debut in September 1984 in the musical *The Tap Dance Kid*. He played the title role. The musical ran until August 1985, and Savion performed in more than 300 shows.

Bates—join him onstage and dance with him. Of course, Willie gets the part.

THE APPRENTICE

The Tap Dance Kid ran on Broadway for almost two years, entertaining audiences for 669 performances before bringing the curtain down for the last time on August 11, 1985. After the actors who played Willie—Alfonso Ribeiro and then Jimmy Tate—moved on to other projects, Savion took over the title role. He began playing Willie in September 1984 and performed in more than 300 shows before the musical closed. In many ways, playing Willie was almost like Savion playing himself. He was just as passionate about dance as his alter ego. Willie is seen tapping in his bedroom, on the sidewalks in his neighborhood, and even on the tram taking him from his Roosevelt Island home to Manhattan and back. In an interview with the magazine *Time for Kids*, Savion was asked where he practiced his tapping. As if transformed into Willie, he replied, "Everywhere. I would dance waiting for a cab, walking, in the shower…"

Performing in *The Tap Dance Kid* at such a young age was a life-changing experience for Savion, scholastically, professionally, and personally. He transferred from Queen of Angels, a Catholic school in Newark, to the Professional Children's School in Manhattan. Never quite comfortable there, he transferred a year later to the East Harlem Performing Arts School. Despite his raw, extraordinary talent, Savion was still only 12 years old. He had so much to learn about dance, about technique, maneuvering around on stage, performing in front of a theater audience. Here, the legendary masters of the medium took the young boy under their tutelage, and Savion welcomed it. Wrote Bruce Weber of Savion in *My Life in Tap*:

> As a dancer he aped his elders, mastering the conventional steps—the shuffle, the paddle and roll, the buck and wing—and fusing them to a youthful enthusiasm and athletic, muscular grace. It would be years before he would begin to develop his own style, but as a dancer, he was, if not yet original, fast and inexhaustible.

Though professional opportunities were exciting, and financially beneficial, they also required Yvette to maneuver her son through the other, more difficult aspects of the entertainment world. Here she would have to find a balance for her child performer in an adult, vice-filled, and fast-paced showbiz lifestyle. It wasn't long before the Glovers would travel abroad, introducing Savion to a whole world outside Newark and Manhattan.

BLACK AND BLUE

A few years after *The Tap Dance Kid's* run ended, Savion was off to Paris, France, to take a role in Claudio Segovia and Héctor Orezzoli's musical revue *Black and Blue*. The show opened at the Theatre Musical de Paris in 1988, with a cast that included three generations of tappers, including Lon Chaney, Jimmy Slyde, Ralph Brown, Bunny Briggs, George Hillman, Dianne Walker (the only woman to dance in the famed Hoofers' Line in the show), Cyd Glover (no relation), and Dormeshia Sumbry.

According to a description of the show on *The Guide to Musical Theatre* Website, *Black and Blue* is:

> ... a celebration of a great and marvelous cultural legacy, the classic African-American tradition of song, dance and music. It is set in the period between the two world wars, the period in Paris where black American artists were given an unusually warm reception. The show reflects a Parisian affection for the exotic. It also has plenty of old-fashioned Hollywood razzle-dazzle. It is a homage to all the spirits of all the legends that created the wonderful period that is *Black and Blue*.

Though Savion took his place on the traditional Hoofers' Line, he did have the opportunity to take a solo turn alongside his mentors on the line. He also performed a "spiffy" duet number with George Hillman. (During the Broadway run, this piece evolved and Savion was joined by Cyd Glover and Sumbry in a breakneck gymnastics-type number dancing up and down a three-step staircase.) Though distractions were few, Savion and Yvette did take a trip to Monte Carlo, the glittering district in the small principality of Monaco. Known for its attraction to the rich and famous, as well as its gambling casino, Monte Carlo also has beautiful beaches, with very relaxed bathing rules. Yvette remembered coming upon a nude beach with Savion in tow and quickly redirecting their afternoon stroll to where the yachts sailed into the protective harbor.

THE SPONGE

It was easier for Yvette to shield her son from the rather free and open world of Europeans than it was with the hoofer legends in the dressing room. Savion spent all his free time hanging around them. Of course they didn't censor their language, and though Yvette did not remove her son from their presence, she kept herself far enough away so she could read her Bible without hearing their conversations, which were often sprinkled with colorful language. Savion was just a permanent fixture, sitting and listening to the old-timers talk. Dianne Walker in *My Life in Tap* said: "Savion was always asking questions, and watching, watching, watching. If Slyde and Chaney were playing cards, Savion would watch them play cards. He just couldn't get enough of those guys." Slyde even gave Savion the nickname "The Sponge" because he was always underfoot, soaking up everything he heard.

Black and Blue eventually moved across the Atlantic Ocean and opened on Broadway on January 26, 1989. Savion reprised his role in the New York production along with most of the original Paris cast. Without consciously realizing it, Slyde, Briggs, Chaney, and the others were passing on the rich dance tradition of tap to this young boy from Newark, New Jersey, who just had to "move," had to "bang," had to have a release for all his energy. The trip to Europe played a part in seeing that the almost lost art of tap was being passed on to ensure its survival. It was also where Savion would meet perhaps the most influential person in his life besides his mother. The beginning of this mentor-protégé relationship would cement Savion's love of tap and his desire to dance forever.

5

Jelly's Last Jam

By the time _Black and Blue_ made its debut in New York at the Minskoff Theatre on January 26, 1989, Savion had danced many times with his tap idols, including Bunny Briggs, Lon Chaney, Ralph Brown, and Jimmy Slyde. These were the legends of hoofin', the men who breathed life into the foot-moving, percussion-sounding fah-da-bop, diggerty-diggerty, clickity-clickity bop that is tap. And Savion loved being around them, absorbing every move, subtle or obvious, that these dance icons could maneuver. They were all very influential and superb teachers of the craft for Savion, but when Gregory Hines came into his life, the evolution of that mentor/friend/father-figure relationship would have more of an impact on the young tapper's life than anyone could have imagined, including Hines.

Described by many as the greatest tap dancer of his generation, Gregory Hines had been tap dancing since the age of three. He learned how to tap from his older brother, Maurice, and was performing professionally with his brother by the time he turned five. Hines, like Savion, spent time around the tap masters of the times, seeing them perform and hanging out with them backstage in between shows. Now, the "legends" were speaking highly and enthusiastically to Hines about Savion and his awesome talent. But Hines was skeptical. Over the years, he had seen many a new young sensation and then been left disappointed. Yet, he was interested enough to see Savion for himself. In the foreword to *My Life in Tap*, Hines shared his recollections of his first encounter—in Paris during a performance of *Black and Blue*:

> It was not enough for me that great living legends like Jimmy Slyde, Bunny Briggs, Lon Chaney, Ralph Brown, Dianne Walker, Buster Brown, and George Hillman had all raved to me about Savion's tap skills and stage presence. No, I had to see for myself.... As he moved out onto the stage, right away I could see ... how cute and adorable he was. Uh-oh, I thought, here we go again. Then he began to dance, and ... all the things I had heard about this young boy were true.... It was all there—the speed, the clarity, the vocabulary, the power (even then he hit the floor hard), and the ease. His tapping would have been impressive for a dancer of any age, but he was ... relaxed and confident onstage, with just that hint of cockiness all the great tap dancers enjoy.

HINES AND GLOVER "TAP"

Hines was so impressed with Savion that while Hines was in Paris he recruited Savion for a part in the motion picture *Tap*. The film focuses on the life of Max Washington (played by Hines), an ex-con whose father owned the Sunny Side of the Street tap dance studio. Washington is a gifted tap dancer, but he chose a life of crime for the quick money. After Max gets out of jail on parole, he takes a room in a hotel across the street from the dance studio. Through the windows of the studio, the audience sees Amy (played by Suzzanne Douglass) and her son Lewis (played by Savion Glover) teaching a dance

Gregory Hines

Arguably one of the greatest tap dancers of all time, Gregory Oliver Hines was born on February 14, 1946, in New York City. His older brother Maurice taught Hines how to dance while he was still just a toddler. Hines had often credited his mother with steering the boys into dance as a way of escaping the ghetto. By the time he was five, Gregory and Maurice, known as the Hines Brothers, were performing professionally. They made their debut at the famed Apollo Theater in Harlem when Hines was just six years old. In a 2001 interview with the Associated Press, Hines described the role dance played in his life: "I don't remember not dancing," Hines said. "When I realized I was alive and these were my parents, and I could walk and talk, I could dance."

While still a preteen, Hines made his Broadway debut with Maurice in the 1954 musical *The Girl in the Pink Tights.* While in his 20s, he had a falling out with Maurice and a brief internal struggle about whether to stay in show business. Hines later reconciled with his brother, and by 1978, the two were dancing on Broadway in the musical revue *Eubie!* Hines was lauded for his performance, winning the Theater World Award and receiving his first Tony nomination. With roles in *Comin' Uptown* and *Sophisticated Ladies*, other theater accolades followed, and soon Hines was branching out into film and television. Over his 50-year career, Hines appeared in more than 20 motion pictures, including *The Cotton Club*, *White Nights*, and *Running Scared.* He also had his own television series, *The Gregory Hines Show*, which aired in 1997–1998, and he played a recurring role on the hit TV series *Will & Grace*.

Throughout his career, Hines received more than a dozen nominations for his work in theater, television, and film. Among his numerous awards were the Tony and Drama Desk awards for Best Actor in *Jelly's Last Jam*. He fulfilled a dream in 2001 by portraying his tap idol William Robinson in Showtime's *Bojangles*. Hines was diagnosed with liver cancer in 2002 and died on August 9, 2003.

In his first feature-length film, *Tap*, Savion Glover played Lewis, a young tap dancer. Gregory Hines was the star of the 1989 movie, and several old-time hoofers appeared as well.

class. On the top floor of the studio is where all the old-time hoofers reside. Most portray themselves in the movie, including Jimmy Slyde, Bunny Briggs, Harold Nicholas, and Dianne Walker. Sammy Davis, Jr., co-stars as Lil' Mo, the best friend of Max's father.

In the role of Lewis, Savion portrays someone much like himself—a young would-be tap dancer who watches and learns from the legends. Like Lewis, Savion had no father in his life, so he looked up to Max/Hines. There are some incredible tap dance sequences in the film, which tries to bridge the gap between the great dancing of the 1950s and the rock and roll music of later decades. A review in the February 1989 issue of *Ebony* magazine said, "While *Tap* spares nothing to showcase the talents of its dancers, it also gives careful treatment to the reasons for tap's decline and the prospects of its revival. At the same time, the film, with its futuristic dance techniques and contemporary scores, advances tap dance into the next century."

Appearing in *Tap* gave Savion the opportunity to experience working on a full-length feature film and provided wider audience exposure for his talent. He had one solo dance scene, a vehicle to reveal all that he had learned up to that point, from tap steps and moves, to technique and stage presence. Savion was also being given the time to continue to learn from the legends who were keeping the art of tap alive. *Tap* was not going to break any box office records or win any major film awards, but it did offer an entertaining look at the art of tap dancing. The movie also forever preserved the memory of some of the greatest tappers in dance history.

A TASTE OF EARLY SUCCESS

Black and Blue had a wonderful run on Broadway, entertaining audiences through 829 performances before closing on January 20, 1991. The 1989 Tony Award nominations reflected the success of the revue, with *Black and Blue* receiving 10 nominations, including Best Musical, Best Choreographer, and Best Actress (Ruth Brown and Linda Hopkins). Savion and old-time hoofer Bunny Briggs also received nominations in the Best Featured Actor category. The evening belonged to *Jerome Robbins' Broadway,* which also received 10 nominations. That show won six Tony Awards, including Best Musical, Best Actor, Best Director, Best Featured Actor, and Best Featured Actress. *Black and Blue,* though, earned Tony Awards for Cholly Atkins, Henry LeTang, Frankie Manning, and Fayard Nicholas (Best Choreography), Ruth Brown (Best Actress), and Claudio Segovia and Héctor Orezzoli (Best Costume Design).

Just for Savion to be nominated in the company of such greats in the theater-dance world was an incredible achievement in his young career. Cholly Atkins was half of a legendary tap dance duo with Charles "Honi" Coles. In the 1960s, Motown founder Berry Gordy brought Atkins to Detroit to create the choreographic routines that became the trademark of groups like The Four Tops, The Temptations, and Diana Ross and the Supremes. Henry LeTang, a successful dancer in his own right, taught some of the greatest talents in American entertainment history, including Gregory and Maurice Hines, Debbie Allen, Bette Midler, Harry Belafonte, Chita Rivera, and Billie Holiday. Fayard Nicholas was the older of the Nicholas Brothers, who tapped their way from the Cotton Club to Broadway and Hollywood. Savion even got some exposure to the music industry from blues singer Ruth Brown, his Tony-winning cast mate. A recording star who had several No. 1 songs in the 1950s, Brown was inducted into the Rock and Roll Hall of Fame in 1993.

FINDING HIS WAY

When Savion was first cast in *The Tap Dance Kid*, he felt that he really knew nothing about being on stage. In *My Life in Tap*, he said:

> I went through all the rehearsals, all the understudy's rehearsals, and what did I know about scripts and scenes and blocking and upstaging and cues and exit lines and all that? I had no idea how to change clothes between scenes in time to get back on....What I learned from *The Tap Dance Kid* was the basics, really the basics. Familiarity with the stage. How to position myself. How to prepare. How to listen. How to react to the audience.

To become more comfortable in his new environment, Savion took it upon himself to explore the theater. He wanted to get familiar with the "nuts and bolts" of the construction of a theater, walking on the catwalks and checking out what goes on backstage as if he worked as a stagehand instead of a performer. He felt he was ready to demystify his environment. Sadly, it was also time for Savion to let go of the "magic" of the theater, time to understand the reality of the business of putting on shows. He also felt as if he was not performing in *The Tap Dance Kid*. Rather, he thought it was just his life up there on stage. "And every night, when we'd take our solo bow, I felt like: These people aren't clapping for me, for Savion; they're clapping for Willie, the Tap Dance Kid," he said. "I never felt like Savion was taking that bow."

When Savion began dancing in *Black and Blue*, he started to feel differently about performing. He had started to find his own "groove" as a dancer and as a performer. Before, when he would come out during a show, he would be trying steps and moves to please the audience. But later, when he hung out with Slyde and Chaney, he got a whole different perspective. Savion explained:

> Just by watching them, I saw it wasn't about pleas-
> ing the audience; it was about expressing yourself.
> It didn't happen right away. You don't just wake up
> and find your voice, your style. It has to develop. But
> during *Black and Blue* was when I started realizing I
> could create my own kind of dance. Up to that point
> all I was doing was dancing.

The time Savion spent as a member of the *Black and Blue* cast also played a part in his own personal growth. He wasn't just hanging around the older guys to learn how to dance. With no father figure in his life, the old-timers were the men who took Savion under their wing. They didn't just teach him about dance and stage presence; they taught him about life, about being a man. They took Savion with them, out to dinners, out to clubs, exposing him to life while under their watchful eyes.

THE MUPPETS LEARN TO TAP

In 1990, Savion caught the attention of the producers of the popular children's television series *Sesame Street*. The award-winning educational series for preschoolers showcased the playful, friendly Muppets (a blend of the words *marionette* and *puppet*) created by master puppeteer Jim Henson. Every day, children tuned in to the show for a learning experience presented through songs, comedy, cartoons, and games. The lessons were introduced by such characters as Big Bird, Elmo, Kermit the Frog, Aloysius Snuffleupagus, and Bert and Ernie, to name a few. The show had human characters as well, including Bob the music teacher and Gina the veterinarian. And a who's who of celebrities have been guests on the show, including Jim Carrey, Bill Cosby, Whoopi Goldberg, Sheryl Crow, Alicia Keys, and Venus Williams.

To have a recurring role on the hugely popular show was a great opportunity for Savion. By 1990, *Sesame Street* was seen by millions of children worldwide, and Savion would have the chance to introduce the art of tap dancing and share with them his joy of the craft. His character's name was also Savion, and he would make periodic appearances on the show in the role of a teacher at another character's (Celina) dance studio. It was his job to teach some of the Muppets, like Big Bird, Elmo, and Snuffleupagus, how to tap dance. Savion stayed a part of *Sesame Street* for five years. He enjoyed working on the show, saying how cool

IN HIS OWN WORDS...

For Savion Glover, tap is all in the sound. As he told an interviewer in 2000:

I dance heavy. Loud. And, I just want to be heard all over the place. My style of dancing is not about the body or the hands or the big finish. It's about the rhythms. It's all natural. A lot of dance schools are caught up into just counting out things—slap, slap, slap, slap, shuffle, slap, shuffle, slap, slap. Instead of all that, I break down the rhythm, skickita goo goo blaa blas—to demonstrate the sound.

and what a nice vibe it had been to be a regular. During his stint, Savion became aware that kids were starting to recognize him on the street, giving him a glimpse into life as a celebrity.

Savion's favorite Muppet was Elmo, the furry red monster with the big orange nose. He liked Elmo because "he was always really curious, just like me," Glover said in a 2002 interview with the *Chicago Sun-Times*. "And just between you and me, Snuffleupagus was pretty uncoordinated. He has four feet and they were all left."

Savion's presence on the show did not go unnoticed by the Young Artist Awards, which honors excellence in performers under the age of 18 who work in television, motion pictures, theater, and music. For his work on *Sesame Street* in the 1992–1993 season, Savion was nominated for a Young Artist Award as Outstanding Youth Host in a TV Magazine, News, or Variety Show. Mario Lopez, star of such television series as *Saved by the Bell* and *The Other Half,* won the award for his appearances on the weekly NBC show *Name Your Adventure.* Still, it was an honor for Savion to be nominated for his work on *Sesame Street.*

PIVOTAL "JELLY" ROLE

While Savion was teaching Big Bird to tap dance, he was polishing his own skills. Opportunity knocked again for Savion to team up with Hines—this time in a Broadway production of *Jelly's Last Jam*—about the life of Jelly Roll Morton (whose real name was Ferdinand Joseph Lamothe). Morton is often called the first true composer of jazz. He made the extraordinary contribution of "bridging nineteenth-century blues, vaudeville song, and ragtime with the small jazz ensembles of the 1920s," according to the *ThinkQuest* Website. Morton, though, was a flamboyant, charismatic jazz pianist who lived hard, denied his racial identity, and died destitute and forgotten in the "colored-only" wing of a Los Angeles hospital.

For the first time in his theatrical career, Savion felt that it was he, rather than the character he was portraying, who was getting the applause and praise from the audience. In *The Tap Dance Kid*, Savion was the third replacement; in *Black and Blue*, though he did have a solo in the show, he was mostly part of an ensemble. Cast opposite Hines, who portrayed Morton as an adult, Savion took on the part of the young Jelly Roll. Professionally, he was now 19 years old and looked more like a young man than a boy on stage. He and Hines had grown closer. Not only was Hines a friend, but he also became the father Savion never had. Hines was often a guest at the Glovers' home, joining them at family barbecues. In *My Life in Tap*, Savion said about his relationship with Hines: "He wasn't like Slyde, who's more a grandfather type, with all the mysterious wisdom he lays on you. For me, knowing Gregory is like knowing you have a pops but not meeting him until you're twenty years old, and it turns out he's been very cool all this time."

JELLY'S ISOLATION DANCE

Onstage, Hines continued to push Savion to be his best, and Savion took up the challenge. In perhaps one of the most electrifying numbers in the show, Hines and Savion shared the stage alone, performing a tap duet that served as a metaphor for the young Morton to cast off his youth. As if involved in a "tap" duel, Savion and Hines challenged each other to match each step and then improve on it. As the show's run continued, the challenges in the number became more and more intense, and longer and longer, pushing each performer to the brink of his ability. Called "Jelly's Isolation Dance," the number became the highlight of the show.

Hines marveled at Savion's ability to tap faster, harder, and cleaner than anyone he had ever seen tap, including himself. For Savion, it was a time when he knew he was assuming the mantle. Of the performances, Savion fondly recalled:

> I would do everything he did, right away, right away, keep spitting back to him what he was handing me, and we'd

Savion Glover and Gregory Hines teamed up again in the 1992 Broadway musical _Jelly's Last Jam_, about the life of the jazz composer Jelly Roll Morton. Savion played the young Jelly Roll. He and Hines performed a duet, more like a tap duel, known as "Jelly's Isolation Dance." It was the highlight of the show.

really be laying it down some nights. It was supposed to be a five-minute number, but it went on longer and longer and longer, we'd go on and on, jamming, and some nights people would just gather in the wings and watch. It was six, seven, eight minutes of joy every performance. And yeah, it felt like he was passing the torch down to me every night. It was humbling. Still is.

6

Bring in 'Da Noise, Bring in 'Da Funk!

For his performance in _Jelly's Last Jam_, Savion Glover received a Drama Desk Award nomination for Outstanding Featured Actor in a Musical. It was his second distinguished award nomination from the world of theater in three years. _Time_ magazine writer William A. Henry III said of Glover and Hines: "Savion Glover, 18, outdoes his own brilliant best in tap-dancing the role of the young Jelly. And as the mature Jelly, Gregory Hines vibrates with the kind of glorious triple-threat talent—as singer, dancer, and actor—that Broadway used to revel in but hardly ever witnesses anymore." The show was critically acclaimed, and it garnered many awards and nominations. The show received a total of 22 Tony and Drama Desk Award nominations, with Gregory Hines winning both in the Best Actor in a Musical category.

The last eight years had been very exciting times for Glover. Starting with his role in _The Tap Dance Kid_, he got to meet and learn from some of the greats in tap-dance history. For his performance in *Black and Blue*, Savion earned the honor of being one of the youngest performers ever nominated for a Tony Award. Before his eighteenth birthday, he had already traveled to Europe, appeared in his first full-length motion picture, and was a cast member of the critically acclaimed children's television show *Sesame Street*. Also at age 18, he earned yet another theatrical award nomination for his work in *Jelly's Last Jam*.

BRANCHING OUT

While working with Slyde, Briggs, Chaney, Hines, and others, Savion was taking what he learned and beginning to develop his own tap style, which he called "free form–hard core" tapping. In July 1990, Savion made his debut as a choreographer at the Apollo Theater with the show *A Night of Tap at the Apollo*. In collaboration with Brenda Bufalino and her American Tap Dance Orchestra, Savion joined Hines, Charles "Honi" Coles, Sandman Simms, The Silver Bells, and others for an evening of dance as part of the New York City Tap Festival. In 1992, Savion became the youngest recipient of a National Endowment for the Arts (NEA) Choreographers' Fellowship grant. Established by Congress in 1965, "the NEA is a public agency dedicated to supporting excellence in the arts, both new and established; bringing the arts to all Americans; and providing leadership in arts education," its Website says.

Savion Glover found joy not only in learning from the old-timers, but also in teaching others. He was also ready to try his hand (or feet) at creating a work that would showcase his own artistic talents and lend a voice to his own expression of tap. During the run of *Jelly's Last Jam*, the show's director, George C. Wolfe, approached Glover to talk about working on a new project with him. He asked the young tapper a hypothetical question—if Glover could do his own show, what would that show be? For Glover, the timing was perfect for the opportunity to explore his own project. He felt that he had

gotten to the point in *Jelly's Last Jam* where he had learned
how to do his own thing and was comfortable enough to step
out on his own and show the world his talent.

THE PUBLIC AS A VENUE

Among his many creative endeavors, Wolfe was the producer
and artistic director of the renowned New York Shakespeare
Festival and the Public Theater from 1993 to 2004. American
theatrical producer and director Joseph Papp founded the
Public Theater in 1954 as a way to make Shakespeare's works
accessible to the public for free. It is "an American theater in
which all the country's voices, rhythms, and cultures con-
verge," the Public's Website says. "The Public Theater produces

George C. Wolfe

The multiple award-winning director George C. Wolfe was born on September
23, 1954, in a "very tight black" segregated community in Frankfort, Kentucky. Wolfe described his childhood as very nurturing. He was told that he
"was magical ... special and extraordinary," allowing him to grow up without
being made to feel inferior. Not until he wanted to see Disney's animated film
101 Dalmatians did he have his first experience with racism, when he was not
permitted to enter the "whites-only" theater.

Instead of becoming bitter or angry about being discriminated against,
Wolfe channeled his energy in a positive direction, striving to achieve excellence in all he did. He developed a love of the theater at an early age and
attended Broadway shows, including a memorable production of *Hello Dolly*.

He began to direct plays in high school. While attending Pomona College in
California, Wolfe gained attention when his play *Up for Grabs* was chosen as
the Pacific Southern Regional winner at the American College Theater Festival.
His next play, *Block Party*, won another award from the festival the following
year. Exposed to so many communities (Asian, Hispanic, gay) while living in
Los Angeles, Wolfe began to use the theater to delve into the social and politi-
cal climate of the times.

Wolfe started to make a name for himself in theater a few years after he
moved to New York in 1979. His play *The Colored Museum* caught the attention of Joseph Papp, the New York Shakespeare Festival and Public Theater

new plays, musicals, productions of Shakespeare, and other classics in its headquarters on Lafayette Street (the former Astor Library, which opened as the Public Theater in 1967 with the world premiere of the musical *Hair*) and at the Delacorte Theater, its permanent summertime home of free Shakespeare in Central Park."

Over its more than 50-year existence, the Public has produced plays and musicals that have won 40 Tony Awards, 135 Obies (the Off-Broadway Theater Awards presented by *The Village Voice*), 38 Drama Desk Awards, and 4 Pulitzer Prizes. The Public has brought more than 40 shows to Broadway, including *That Championship Season*, *A Chorus Line*, and *The Pirates of Penzance*. Glover's show would be

founder and director, and earned Wolfe an award from the Dramatists Guild. Wolfe's breakthrough production as a director was *Jelly's Last Jam*, which earned an impressive 11 Tony Award nominations and starred Gregory Hines and Savion Glover.

In 1993, Wolfe moved away from working on plays that mostly had an African-American theme when he directed writer Tony Kushner's award-winning AIDS drama, *Angels in America: The Millennium Approaches* on Broadway. The critically acclaimed show won Wolfe the coveted Tony Award for Best Director. The next year, he directed *Perestroika*, the second part of *Angels in America*. In 1996, Wolfe reteamed with Savion Glover to co-create and direct the highly energetic *Bring in 'Da Noise, Bring in 'Da Funk*, for which he won his second Best Director Tony.

Two years after Papp's death in 1991, Wolfe took the reins as artistic director and producer of the New York Shakespeare Festival and the Public Theater. He remained actively involved until he stepped down in 2004 to pursue projects in a new medium: film. In 2005, he made his film-directing debut with Ruben Santiago-Hudson's semiautobiographical screenplay *Lackawanna Blues*. The movie was shown at the Sundance Film Festival before it ran on HBO. Bringing his characteristic energy and work ethic to the screen has just been a new way for Wolfe to weave his stories for audiences who have enjoyed his vision of life.

added to that impressive list in 1996. Wolfe's position at the Public gave him an unprecedented artistic voice in American theater. Approaching Glover to develop a new project would give the tap sensation a place to bring it all together.

PUTTING IT TOGETHER

After Glover completed his commitment to the Broadway run and road tour of *Jelly's Last Jam*, he and Wolfe went to work on the new show. Wolfe had asked Glover with whom he wanted to work, and it was as if Glover had been subconsciously preparing for this moment. He did have some people in mind whom he wanted to get involved in the creative process, some he had already worked with and others whose work he admired. One was poet Reg E. Gaines. Glover had seen Gaines reciting some of his poems on MTV's *Spoken Word*. His work has been described as raw, street-style poetry. In an interview for the Artists Network, Gaines explained how he became interested in this kind of poetry and why he writes in such a "raw" style of expression:

> I got into this because I felt voiceless. I probably never would have started writing poetry if I hadn't gone to the Nuyorican Poets Cafe. The first night I was there I saw Willie Perdomo reading ... and he goes off in the language I had heard on the streets. I was like, damn, I didn't know that was poetry. I thought, I gotta go up there and do that; I wasn't thinking anything about writing poetry, I was just thinking I wanna go up there on that stage and do that. So Willie informed me just by reading his poem, that up to that point in my life, and I had been alive at least three decades at that point, that I had been voiceless my entire life.

Glover did not know Gaines, but he wanted to meet him and have him involved in the show's conceptualization.

Glover also approached Ann Duquesnay, a singer, composer, and actor who had been in the cast of *Jelly's Last Jam*. In *My Life in Tap*, Glover recalled how Duquesnay had left a memorable impression on him: "I remember I'd heard her sing at something my mom was doing, a gospel revue at the Victory Theater. She sang this song, man, 'Believe in Yourself,' and that was it for me. I didn't know her back then. But I remembered her singing it from I don't know how many years ago."

Glover recruited several black artists, including young dancers he knew through the years: Baakari Wilder, Dulé Hill, Vincent Bingham, and Jimmy Tate, who had been Willie in *The Tap Dance Kid* before Glover took over the role. Collaborating on the musical writing were Duquesnay, Zane Mark, and Daryl Waters. Wolfe had worked with all of these people on other projects, and he was quite excited at the prospect of bringing everyone together to create a new and different work for the Public Theater. Glover came to the project with the desire to explore and develop a work that combined the ideas of rhythm and history. He also wanted to tell the world about the legendary hoofers like Slyde, Chaney, Green, and Briggs. Glover felt the story that needed to be told was a history, because as he said in his autobiography, "that's what tap is, that's what tap carries, history, and not just the history of tap but what was going on while tap dancing was going on."

CREATING THE STORY

It was Gaines who first broached the idea of putting together a story about the history of racism as told through Glover's feet. It was an elusive and rather abstract concept to several of the performers who gathered to brainstorm with Glover and Wolfe. At one point, Glover tried to explain what he envisioned as bringing the concepts of "the noise" and "the funk" to life. Those words were not just conceptual terms to Glover;

Savion Glover (center) and the cast members of *Bring in 'Da Noise, Bring in 'Da Funk* performed a scene from the show at the Tony Awards in June 1996. George C. Wolfe, the director of *Jelly's Last Jam*, had approached Glover during that show and asked Savion what he would do if he could do his own show. From that, *Noise/Funk* emerged.

they were a reflection of an attitude, more easily expressed through movement than language. In *My Life in Tap*, Gaines describes the strategy session:

> We all sat down at a round table. There were maybe twenty people, and there was a tape recorder going, and George asked, 'What does "bring the noise and bring the funk" mean?' And the older people there were all saying, 'Oh, the funky chicken, and James Brown.' And then Savion said, 'Nah, nah. Y'all don't get it. Say me and Dulé, we want to go out dancing

one night. We're gonna be like, "Yo, bro, we gonna go out and *dance* tonight, and we gonna bring the *noise!*"... And I took the tape home and listened to it, and I thought, this could be the whole show, defining what that means.

At home that night, Gaines took out a piece of paper and wrote down, "Bring the noise, bring the funk, bring the best you got." To him that phrase meant doing your best, with the word "noise" defined as *excellence*.

The script Gaines wrote became the foundation for the show, with Duquesnay, Mark, and Waters creating the music and Duquesnay, Gaines, and Wolfe writing the lyrics. Glover and others worked on creating the dance around Gaines's story. Duquesnay recalled the challenge of composing and the fun of being free to draw from her own background as part of the creative process. She said, "We started work with no script, no title, no nothing.... I even put my own nickname into a song, as well as a memory of my mother shouting down at me to come in from a window in our five-story walkup in Harlem when I was a little girl, 'Mootsie, come on up here girl.' "

Gaines's script was filled with passions like anger and defiance as well as sensitive lyric and poetic expressions—all to convey the core spirit of noise and funk through the history of blacks in America. His words were given a voice through multitalented actor Jeffrey Wright (*Angels in America*), who played the role of "da voice" in the show. And though the original concept was to tell the story of the history of racism in America through Glover's feet, it became a story about how blacks *responded* to that racism through tap. Of his "feet tappin' gift," Wolfe said about Glover: "From generation to generation, tap dancers taught each other their steps. The old-timers passed their information on to Savion, and it landed in his feet, his being and his soul."

Savion Glover leads a master tap class for hopeful dancers during the run of *Bring in 'Da Noise, Bring in 'Da Funk*. Representatives of the Public Theater were observing the class to identify and develop talented dancers for future companies and tours of the musical.

Just as the script, the music, and a title for what would become *Bring in 'Da Noise, Bring in 'Da Funk* all needed to be created, so too did the dance numbers. It was a major step in Glover's career to take on the choreography of a show that might end up on Broadway. And rather than try to develop specific dances for a specific scene, the creative process involved taking ideas, sounds, and movements and creating a scene from them. For example, instead of trying to "create" a dance in a factory to convey an "industrial" feel, Glover and his cast mates "played" with their creative talents until the scene emerged. They were not restricted by some preconceived idea or plan as to what they would do each day.

Glover described one such session with bucket drummers J.R. Crawford and Larry Wright:

> We had J.R. and Larry in there ... and they could just get a sound out of anything. A pot, a pan, the button on the top of your hat. So they were in rehearsal one day playing the walls, and I was just fooling around, swinging from a pipe, and my leg comes up and J.R., he starts to play the bottom of my shoe. And George was there, and he looked up, and he said, "Can you do a routine where he plays the bottom of your shoe?"

Much of the show's six scenes developed without a plan, instead evolving from the creative process that occurred when Glover and the others met each day, improvising as they went along. Gaines would watch what was unfolding in the studio and then go off and write. Wolfe would watch, listen, ask questions, and let the cast experiment. Everybody was loose and relaxed, working in an atmosphere more akin to hanging out, instead of enduring the rigors of a more staid, typical rehearsal environment. What started out as a Public Theater workshop quickly took on the look, sound, and feel of a Broadway-bound musical.

TAP/RAP DISCOURSE ON THE STAYING POWER OF THE BEAT

Bring in 'Da Noise, Bring in 'Da Funk takes the audience on a journey that begins with the slave ships arriving along America's shores, through the exploitation of black labor in the factories, the high-society period that was the Harlem Renaissance, and up to the present hip-hop street life of contemporary black America. The scene "In 'Da Beginning" takes the audience through the slave era; "Urbanization" is about the scene in Chicago; "Street Corner Symphony" deals with the new inner-city period. One of the show's most interesting moments is the scene called "Taxi," in which Glover, Vincent Bingham, Jimmy

Backstage at _Bring in 'Da Noise, Bring in 'Da Funk_, Savion Glover sits on a grate that is lighted from below. The musical took the audience on a journey that began with slave ships arriving at America's shores and continued to the present day of contemporary black America.

Tate, and Baakari Wilder dance out the frustrations of black men, all in different attire, who are trying without success to flag down a taxicab. The showcase number, "Noise/Funk," highlights the new hittin' style of Glover and his dance cast mates through the creation of "music" via the sounds of tap shoes and other objects like paint buckets and chains.

What Glover and company did was create the beat using everything at their disposal—shoes and bucket drums, pots and pans, trash can lids—producing the pulsating beat and tap complement to the story. In fact, tap dance is the principal artistic expression used to take the audience on this African-American journey. While the music and dancing were loud and fast-paced, the sound was also new, resembling rap music and hip-hop, the kind of sound that the black youth made their signature.

To all the noise, funk, rhythm, and tap, *Bring in 'Da Noise, Bring in 'Da Funk,* subtitled "A Tap/Rap Discourse on the Staying Power of the Beat," premiered at the Public Theater on November 15, 1995, to strong reviews. *New York Times* critic Ben Brantley wrote, "In finding a resonant individuality in each number, peculiar both to its historical origins and to the dancers performing it, the show restores emotional content to show-biz choreography in ways currently unmatched on Broadway stages.... Its rhythms will continue to pulse in your bloodstream long after the show is over." Performances ran at the Public until January 28, 1996. But the show didn't end. It moved uptown to New York City's Theater District, to the Ambassador Theatre, to Broadway. Glover was about to embark on one of the most professional and personal journeys of his life—all at the tender age of 22.

7

Taking Tap to the Next Level

On April 25, 1996, just five months after its stage debut at the Public Theater, *Bring in 'Da Noise, Bring in 'Da Funk* opened at the Ambassador Theatre on Broadway. The Ambassador, built in 1921, has seen many a Broadway luminary and theatrical production grace its stage in its more than 80-year history. Shows like *The Lion in Winter, The Diary of Anne Frank, Godspell,* and *You're a Good Man, Charlie Brown* entertained audiences young and old. Eighteen years before Savion Glover hit his first tap step on the Ambassador's stage, his mentor Gregory Hines had revived his tap career with a performance in the musical revue *Eubie!* on that very stage.

Glover and company picked up where they left off at the Public, wowing audiences and critics alike. *Bring in 'Da Noise, Bring in 'Da Funk* was fresh; it was different, unlike anything seen on Broadway before. Glover, Wolfe, Gaines, and the rest of the show's collaborators seemed to have tapped into something unique, and the public was just dazzled by it all. *Harlem Live* writer Kerly Suffren described the experience this way:

> The show illustrated music at its best, capturing minds and stealing souls to describe their point. The tools used were different in each dance. They were a form of art consisting of the people, tap shoes, pots, pans, rope, metal, wood, buckets and any [material] that can be found to produce music. That was unique. Much of the equipment used in the dances was not high-tech and basically were household items that can be found anywhere. The actors took advantage of this and expressed themselves using the instruments they were given.

Overnight it seemed, *Bring in 'Da Noise, Bring in 'Da Funk* changed the impression of what Broadway theater had been up to that point: serious dramas, or lavish musicals in a predominantly white man's world. The Glover-Wolfe collaboration opened the theater up to the hip-hop, rap culture, bringing the dance and music of young black artists to an older, mostly white theatergoing public.

ARTICULATING A THESIS

Aside from its fresh, entertaining, and hip look, sound, and feel, *Bring in 'Da Noise, Bring in 'Da Funk* hit a more serious nerve with some in the black community. It gave a voice to the less-than-favorable treatment of blacks in America's history. In the *African-American Review,* writer Elmo Terry-Morgan echoed the more serious view of its importance:

> *Noise/Funk* does what few plays on Broadway, and even fewer Black plays on The Great White Way, have been allowed to do: articulate a thesis. As if

collaborating on a history book, the creators of *Noise/Funk* brainstormed the scope of their research, organized it into chronological chapters, and, quite importantly, determined its purpose. This last places *Noise/Funk* squarely in the history and tradition of Black Theatre. The preferred style of blending a didactic purpose with entertainment values is a long-standing tradition in the history of African-American dramatic art.

Glover and Wolfe had achieved their goal: bring the noise, bring the funk to the people, and bring tap to the forefront of dance. Toward the end of the show, Glover came onstage for a solo dance. For him, it was the melding of the historical context of tap in black culture and the personal connection for him with the ones who taught him about this thing called tap. The number was called "Green, Chaney, Buster, Slyde," for the old hoofers who were "tap." During the piece, Glover danced in the styles of his mentors and idols and spoke about what these people had meant to him. It was also the moment when Glover took his place, deservedly, among them, announcing that tap would not disappear; rather that with his heroes' help, and his hard work and natural talent, Glover had found where he fit in this rich history of tap. He was up to the challenge and was just getting started.

IN HIS OWN WORDS...

Savion Glover has no doubts about the future of tap. In an interview with *The Philadelphia Inquirer*, he said:

> Tap dance is like air. It's alive. It will be here and continue to be here. The youth coming up is interested in dance now, and they're coming to the shows. That's a blessing for those of us who create.

ACHIEVING RECOGNITION

There is no doubt that the success of *Bring in 'Da Noise, Bring in 'Da Funk* catapulted Glover into the spotlight, giving him star status in the entertainment industry. If people outside the dance world had not known about the young sensation before *Noise/Funk,* they certainly did after he took Broadway by storm. Though there had been a trickle of prestigious theater award nominations in his young career, Glover received a tidal wave of them with *Bring in 'Da Noise, Bring in 'Da Funk.*

Several theater awards are presented each year. Among them are the Drama Desk Awards, which honor achievements in all New York theater productions; the *Village Voice* Obie Awards for the best of off-Broadway; the Theater World Award, which celebrates debut performances of promising personalities who have appeared on Broadway; and the Tony Awards, which honor excellence in Broadway productions. When the Tony nominations were announced on May 2, 1996, *Bring in 'Da Noise, Bring in 'Da Funk* received nine, including Best Musical, Best Choreography, Best Director (Musical), Best Actor (Musical), and Best Featured Actress (Musical). The choreography and actor nominations were for Glover.

"NOISE/FUNK" IN THE SPOTLIGHT

Glover and company filed into the Majestic Theater on Broadway on the evening of June 2, 1996, along with hundreds of other members of the theater community, in anticipation of an unforgettable night. The fiftieth anniversary of the Tonys was not without preshow controversies, despite Broadway attendance being at an all-time high and ticket sales exceeding $430 million for the season. Some producers and stars felt there were snubs by the nominating committee. Legendary singer, actress, and stage star Julie Andrews stunned the theater world when she announced that she was refusing her nomination for Best Actress for the musical *Victor/Victoria.* Hers was the show's only nomination, whereas the rest of the cast and crew were "egregiously overlooked."

The awards show's host, Nathan Lane—best known for his comedic roles onstage, including *The Producers* and *The Odd Couple*, and a Tony Award recipient himself—joked about the controversies by welcoming the audience to the "Tabloid Tonys." Though the show *Rent* received the most nominations (10) and was competing in many of the same categories as *Bring in 'Da Noise, Bring in 'Da Funk*, Glover and company certainly shared the spotlight with the evening's other big winners. *Noise/Funk* co-creator George Wolfe won the Tony for Best Director (Musical), Ann Duquesnay won for Best Featured Actress (Musical), and Glover, at just 22, won the Tony for Best Choreography. Making the moment that much more special, Glover's mentor and friend Gregory Hines was there to congratulate him. In all, *Bring in 'Da Noise, Bring in 'Da Funk* garnered four Tony Awards (the fourth was for Best Lighting Design).

Aside from his big night at the Tony Awards, Glover earned other accolades for his choreography of *Noise/Funk*, picking up

The Tony Awards Medallion

Each year, the Tony Awards are presented by the American Theater Wing to celebrate excellence in the theater. Established in 1947 in honor of the late actress, director, and producer Antoinette Perry, the first awards evening was a gala black-tie event that included dinner, dancing, and entertainment. No official Tony Award, however, was given out in 1947 or 1948. During those two years, winners were presented with a scroll, along with a cigarette lighter for the men and a compact for the women.

In 1949, United Scenic Artists, a designers union, promoted a contest to secure a design for the award. The winning entry, which was submitted by Herman Rosse, portrayed a disk-shaped medallion with the images of the comedy and tragedy masks on one side and a profile of Perry on the other. In 1968, the medallion began to be mounted on a black pedestal framework. At the conclusion of the awards ceremony, each Tony statuette is numbered and engraved with the winner's name.

George C. Wolfe and Savion Glover celebrated backstage after winning Tony Awards on June 2, 1996, for *Bring in 'Da Noise, Bring in 'Da Funk*. Wolfe won as Best Director, and Glover took the honor for Best Choreography. The following year, Glover would form his own dance company called Not Your Ordinary Tappers, or NYOTs.

Drama Desk and Outer Critics Circle awards in that category. In April, Glover had also received the prestigious Choreographer of the Year Award from *Dance Magazine*, so 1996 was shaping up to be a great year for the young tap dance phenom. But *Bring in 'Da Noise, Bring in 'Da Funk* meant more to Glover than success and stardom. He knew from the beginning, the inception of the project, that the show would have everything he had learned, off stage and on. It would have everything he had learned about dance, stage presence, the performance, and the audience. For him, *Bring in 'Da Noise, Bring in 'Da Funk* was like giving birth to himself as an artist, as a student of the art. Said Glover in his autobiography:

> Before *Noise/Funk*—when I was doing *Tap Dance Kid* and *Black and Blue* and *Jelly's*—that was like being pregnant, nourishing this baby with all the knowledge I had. And then I just put together all this information, and this inspiration, from all those years hanging out, with my mom and brothers, and with Slyde and Chaney and Chuck, all these years of being in the world. And then I took this killer cast, and we just put it down. So that's what *Noise/Funk* was to me, introducing myself to the world. My first baby. Me.

KEEPING IT GOING

Glover left *Bring in 'Da Noise, Bring in 'Da Funk* in July 1996. On March 7, 1997, one of his mentors, Chuck Green, died. The melodious sounds from one of the "original" hoofers, who attached bottle caps to his shoes with tar and danced for coins as a kid in Fitzgerald, Georgia, went silent. Green had toured and performed well into the 1990s. That's how much he loved tap. In the fall, a memorial service for Green was held at St. Peter's Church in Manhattan. Glover was there. So was Jimmy Slyde. After the service the two sat, Glover mostly listening, Slyde doing most of the talking. Glover had looked upon the old hoofers like Slyde, Green, Chaney, and others as if they were his guardians, the keepers of the secrets of tap as well as its teachers. Slyde had the joy of watching Glover blossom and grow into one of the best tap dancers the world had ever seen. Slyde had toured with Glover, performed with him, and often doled out advice and shared his innermost thoughts freely with "The Sponge."

Glover recalled what Slyde said to him that day: "Right now, where we've taken tap, we got to keep it there, keep it in the public eye, keep it seen, keep it on TV, keep it onstage, keep something happening for the dance." Then Slyde told Glover he needed to go and create a new cologne, calling it Da Funk. Glover didn't know if Slyde was joking with him or not, but the more he thought later about what Slyde had said to him in the church, the more he wondered if it was more a metaphor for going out and creating his own tap "cologne," to keep the art of tap alive and moving forward. And Glover felt ready to take his work to the next level. He was ready to have another "baby."

THE NEXT STEP

With the success of *Bring in 'Da Noise, Bring in 'Da Funk* and an overall feeling of personal and professional growth behind him, Glover decided to take the next step forward in his career. In 1997, he formed his own dance company, aptly named Not Your Ordinary Tappers or NYOTs (pronounced "nots"). The group came together through family and friendships over the years. Glover's brother Abron, his cousin Omar Edwards, and friends Jason Samuels and Ayodele Casel (the only woman in the company) were members of the original troupe.

Glover decided to debut his NYOTs in their first show, *Savion and Friends*, at the Crossroads Theater Company, the nation's premier African-American theater, in New Brunswick, New Jersey. Glover had a long relationship with the Crossroads throughout its rich and sometimes troubled history. "Founded in 1978 by Rutgers acting graduates [Ricardo] Khan and L. Kenneth Richardson, Crossroads quickly rose to national prominence for its development of African-American plays and artists," Peggy McGlone wrote in *The Star-Ledger*. "In its heyday, it produced four shows and a play-reading festival each season, attracting the likes of August Wilson, Avery Brooks, Ntozake Shange and Rita Dove." Among its accolades, Crossroads was the recipient of the 1999 Tony Award for Outstanding Regional Theatre in the United States and the National Governors Association Award for Distinguished Service in the Arts.

After their performance at the Crossroads, Glover took the NYOTs on tour. He also brought tap into the spotlight in other entertainment outlets, gaining incredible exposure for the art and himself. He began picking projects that would expand the audience size for tap beyond theatergoers. Along with the NYOTs, Glover choreographed a piece for the televised season opener of ABC's *Monday Night Football* on September 2, 1997. On the show-opening video, Hank Williams, Jr., sang his signature ditty "Are You Ready for Some Football," to which he added the words "Bring on 'Da Game." Joining Williams, Glover and company tapped out a four-minute routine for a broadcast audience in the millions. Glover could also be seen on Puff Daddy and the Family's music video *All About the Benjamins*, which ran on MTV. Glover was definitely reaching much larger audiences.

BROADCAST EXPOSURE

Having taken tap beyond the stages of New York, in 1998, Glover experimented in yet another medium—film. Collaborating with director Rob Cohen, producer Fred Caruso, and composer Mark Adler, Glover took his first film choreographer production credit for the HBO docudrama *The Rat Pack*, starring Ray Liotta, Joe Mantegna, Angus Macfadyen, and Don Cheadle. The film takes a behind-the-scenes look at the

In 1998, Savion Glover appeared in *The Wall*, a Showtime film about three men who never returned home from the Vietnam War. Here, some of the artists involved in the film gathered before its premiere at the National Museum of American History in Washington, D.C. They were (from left) actor Michael DeLorenzo; musician Graham Nash, who performed an original song for the film; Ruby Dee, who played Glover's grandmother; and Glover.

interaction of the stars labeled the Rat Pack in the 1960s—Frank Sinatra, Peter Lawford, Dean Martin, and Sammy Davis, Jr.

Glover also appeared in a Showtime film titled *The Wall*, which traces the stories of three men who never made it back home from the Vietnam War and the three mementos of theirs left at the Vietnam Veterans War Memorial in Washington, D.C. Glover joined an all-star cast that included *Stand and Deliver* actor Edward James Olmos and legendary actress Ruby Dee. In the segment called "The Badge," Glover plays a young man who enlists in the military as his grandfather and father had before him. His grandmother, played by Dee, gives him a badge, the family heirloom for good luck, before he goes off to war.

With a few cable TV projects behind him, Glover took on the challenge of being the executive producer and star of his first special, *Savion Glover's Nu York*, which aired on ABC. Glover choreographed the production, and he tried his hand at composing the musical score. Joining him in the production were Stevie Wonder, Puff Daddy and the Family, and Silk Suits.

Glover's new projects, which were not exclusively dance, did not keep him from performing. In September 1998, he performed for President Clinton in *Savion Glover's Stomp, Slide and Swing: In Performance at the White House*, which was shown on PBS. He was also the emcee of the show, which celebrated the diversity and history of tap dance in America. Glover and the NYOTs provided the modern style of tap for which Glover is noted. Following them onstage was 70-year-old Jimmy Slyde, whose dancing reflected the elegant origins of tap, and eight-year-old prodigy Cartier Williams of Washington, D.C. Donny Golden—the first American to win international Irish step-dancing competitions—and some of his young students demonstrated a few reels and jigs, and their band played an Irish-style tune composed in Arkansas. Two duets of Lindy Hoppers exhibited a combination of social dance and tap, and Bebe Neuwirth and Karen Ziemba performed two numbers from the hit musical *Chicago*, showcasing Bob Fosse's signature style of Broadway tap.

DID YOU KNOW?

Savion Glover has not used only music to accompany his tap. During the finale of the 1998 NAACP Image Awards, the world-renowned poet, writer, and activist Yolande Cornelia "Nikki" Giovanni, Jr., read a part of her poem "But Since You Finally Asked" from her book *The Selected Poems of Nikki Giovanni*. In the background, Glover tapped to her recitation.

DOING WHAT YOU LOVE

Performing has always been Glover's favorite part of being an artist—that, and wanting to bring tap to the world and transform it into something hip for contemporary artists like himself. Throughout the rest of the 1990s, Glover continued to perform around the country, teach classes, and create new shows, new ways to push himself in his craft. The decade had been an enormously creative and professionally satisfying time for Glover, and he would look to the new millennium as an opportunity to take what he loved to yet greater heights.

8

Stomp, Shimmy,
Fuh-duh-Bap!

Savion Glover closed out the 1990s with another public show-ing of his craft with *Savion Glover/Downtown: Live Commu-nication* at the historic Variety Arts Theater in the East Village of New York City. The show ran for more than four weeks in the spring of 1999 with Glover and his NYOTs Ayodele Casel, Omar Edwards, Abron Glover, and Jason Samuels taking cen-ter stage. A variety of guest dancers and musicians performed during the show's run, including Baakari Wilder and Chance Taylor. One highlight was the duet by Glover and Casel, who tapped to a musical rendition of "Cheek to Cheek." Wrote *New York Times* critic Jennifer Dunning of Glover's performance:

> He is capable of the most breathtakingly light, deli-cately nuanced and articulated footwork, displayed in a playful and excitingly competitive show-stopping duet with a triangle-playing Eli Fountain. And there is

considerable cerebral pleasure to Mr. Glover's probing of the music, burrowing into it—and the ground—with footwork that digs rather than skims or bounds from the floor. His upper body hunched, he seems to be searching his dancing feet for the heart of the music, effectively drawing a curtain around himself as he does.

Glover was having a good time, enjoying his work and bringing his art to a wider audience than ever before. Going into the new millennium, his focus would remain on creating performances in tap that would push the boundaries beyond what had been done in the past, working with the legends who brought him into their inner circle and who he knew never really got their proper recognition, and continuing to be involved in other artistic mediums.

BRING IN 'DA COOL

Glover never lost the enjoyment he had felt as a preteen dancing at festivals with tap cool cats like Lon Chaney, Jimmy Slyde, Chuck Green, and Bunny Briggs, and, of course, Aunt Dianne (Dianne Walker). He always appreciated spending time with these seasoned professionals, watching, listening, and learning from them, and that did not change once he began to carve out his own prominence as a tapper and choreographer. In a 2000 interview, Glover said, "I've changed my whole angle for dance. I'm moving towards moving back rather than hanging out with my peers. I'm reaching back to older dudes for a second."

His next project was going to include some of those legends joining him onstage, in a work that could be labeled a dance performance as well as a musical concert. In December 1999, Glover brought a prelude of his new show, *Savion! In Concert: Footnotes*, to the New Jersey Performing Arts Center for a one-night performance. The show starred four generations of tappers, from Glover to James "Buster" Brown, Jimmy Slyde, and Dianne Walker, to young protégé Cartier A. Williams, now 10 years old. "'It's about how I learned from my pioneers,'" Glover said about the show. In March 2000, he took the show on a seven-week nationwide tour that included stops in Los Angeles, San Francisco, Chicago, and Boston. Describing the show for *Dance Magazine*, Pamela Diamond wrote:

> The concert's sections flowed into each other like the hues of a sunset: In fiery orange, Glover was all over the stage as if its space couldn't contain him.... A light-hearted solo by 10-year-old whiz kid and Glover protégé Cartier Williams led to a tongue-in-cheek game of one-upmanship with Glover. At one point a special sound box under the stage made even the tiniest trembling of Glover's toes carry all the rumbling presage of an earthquake, echoing patterns under the floor until they became a drumming flood of repeating rhythms. The second half of the program shed the steamy "pows" for more "ooh-yeah," cool blue tones and slow sensuous rhythms. Glover opened with a soft-shoe sand dance, then segued the show into a series of solos by three other tap legends. Buster Brown showed that his shimmies still are as potent as his humor; Jimmy Slyde slurped across the floor as if gliding over ice; and the elegant intricacies of Dianne Walker's sophisticated tap moves proved as effervescent as champagne.

During a performance of the show in Los Angeles, Glover's mentor and friend Gregory Hines was in the audience. Glover and the other dancers persuaded Hines to come up onstage, where he treated the audience to an impromptu performance, making the magical concert even more special. By now, Glover was doing his own tap thing, and Hines truly enjoyed being entertained by his protégé. The tour's ultimate success rested on the fact that all the participants came out to have a good time and share their love of tap. None of them had to prove themselves, and at the same time they were getting their due.

2000'S THE CHARM

The year 2000 was a busy one for Glover, creatively and professionally. Along with the success of *Footnotes*, his autobiography, *Savion: My Life in Tap*, was also published in 2000. Written in collaboration with *New York Times* national cultural correspondent Bruce Weber, Glover tells the reader about his extraordinary journey, from his introduction to the world of tap as a young artist all the way to the triumphant success of his hit Broadway show, *Bring in 'Da Noise, Bring in 'Da Funk*. Though Glover always let his feet express his sheer joy of tap, the book gave him another means to express that joy—through words. In *The New York Times Book Review*, Simon Rodenberg wrote in his review of *Savion: My Life in Tap*:

> This is a book full of love—for family, for teachers and for art. It is also an education—about tap, and, as Glover writes, about how to be: "Whatever you do, dancing or whatever, you got to hit. Don't sleep on it. Just hit. Because for me, dancing is like life. The lessons of one are the lessons of the other."

> These are perfect lessons for young adolescents, who will appreciate the injunction to "hit," and whose parents will appreciate the creative discipline of this rebellion. Glover shows his readers how to bring the noise and the funk with the force of history. … A caveat: it will be the precocious 10-year-old who can deal with all the vocabulary words in this book. But it will be the rare 10-year-old who is not inspired to be precocious by Savion Glover's story.

Savion Glover (center) portrayed Mantan in the satiric film *Bamboozled*, directed by Spike Lee. In the film, Glover's character is a tapper who agrees to star in a TV variety show called *Mantan: The New Millennium Minstrel Show*.

In the fall, controversial director Spike Lee released his film *Bamboozled*, which writer Veronica Mixon at Hollywood.com called "a funny, outrageous tale that recalls America's terrible racial past while challenging the choices of both blacks and whites that work in the television industry at the present." Lee approached Glover to take on the part of a struggling tapper who agrees to star in *Mantan: The New Millennium Minstrel Show*, a TV comedy-variety program. Glover was enthusiastic about working with Lee and appreciated that the script dealt with a part of history that was not so favorable to blacks. And though Glover knew about the minstrels because of his own background in theater, he was not aware of how extensive racial stereotyping had been. Lee had Glover study minstrel works that Glover did not know had ever been made, including cartoons. Said Glover, "I thought I'd seen every cartoon ever made. I never imagined that [society] could do that."

THE STAGE IS THE PLACE

Despite his ventures into other media to showcase his artistic talent, the stage is where Glover is most at home performing. Over the last six years, Glover has also continued to teach, sometimes while on tour with one of his concerts, and sometimes as a guest faculty member at the Broadway Dance Center, the place where it all began for him nearly 25 years ago.

In 2002, Glover traveled to Utah to perform at Abravanel Hall in Salt Lake City as part of the Olympic Arts Festival, sponsored by the host city of the 2002 Olympic Winter Games. Wrote *Deseret News* staff writer Diane Urbani of Glover's one-night sold-out performance:

> With a saxophone's wind blowing behind him, Glover's amplified soles thundered hard into his opener, a dance he called "an extorted version of 'The Star-Spangled Banner.'" Then on came the members of Ti Dii, his nine partners, flooding the stage with their fluid bodies. Glover stepped to the back row, even offstage at times, but his presence, as a kind of guide through the world of 21st-century tap, pervaded the auditorium throughout the show.

According to Urbani, the audience cheered throughout the show, having as good a time watching Glover as he had dancing.

Still, Glover seemed to be creating less. On August 9, 2003, his dear friend Gregory Hines died. The loss was immensely personal for Glover; at the same time his art, his dance medium, had lost one of the greatest dancers to ever grace the hardwoods. It was Hines's death that seemed to spur Glover back into revitalizing his work full force. His first show *Improvography* (improvisation by choreography), a term coined by Hines, opened in the winter of 2003. Of the show's name, Glover said, "That's his word and that played a part. I wanted to pay tribute to him ... my father, best friend, brother, guru, mentor."

If Savion had felt a strong duty to keep tap alive and vital before Hines's death, he had to have felt it even more afterward. As Brian Seibert wrote for *The Village Voice*:

> Glover's sense of responsibility goes way beyond teaching younger dancers. He presents tap as a serious discipline, stomping to pieces any limiting associations with old Hollywood or Broadway razzle-dazzle. "I plan to brainwash an entire generation," he once told an interviewer.... He's not only concerned with correcting the popular conception of tap, though; he actually wants to make the form popular again, thrust it back in the mainstream, where it was in the '30s, when it acquired those limiting associations. He wants to bring it into rock arenas, Yankee Stadium, TV, and the movies. Other art forms, he points out, happen every night. Why not tap?

Glover's new dance company, Ti Dii, was different from his previous troupes. In Ti Dii (pronounced "tie dye"), the company was multiracial, with half its members women. Glover's protégé Cartier Williams and Michelle Dorrance were just two of the dancers who came onstage in the second half of the show to demonstrate their own styles of tap. As for Glover, besides his bust-loose, frenzied hittin'-the-floor tapping, he also sang. In some shows, he sang "The Way You Look Tonight," others it was "Nature Boy."

In 2004, Glover took a short break from touring to choreograph and direct a musical, *Timmy the Great*, for the Tribeca

Savion Glover (right) rehearses with his dance troupe, Ti Dii, before the opening of *Improvography* in 2003. The name of the show (improvisation by choreography) was a term coined by Gregory Hines, and the show served as a tribute to him.

Theater Festival in New York City. The show was based on the book *King Timmy the Great*, by Sandra Hochman and Tad Danielak, and it followed the story of nine-year-old King Timmy, who radicalizes the world by turning kids into grown-ups and grown-ups into kids. The show was so popular that the two engagements sold out and had a waiting list for tickets.

BRING IN DA BACH!

In 2005, Glover produced *Improvography II*, a concert evening of jazz music and tap dancing. Joining him again was his dance company, now called Chapter I, along with his long-time musicians Tommy James, Brian Grice, Patience Higgins, and Andy McCloud, known as The Otherz. Once again, Cartier Williams joined Glover, as did dancers Maurice Chestnut and Ashley DeForest. Of the group, Glover said, "Each of us

Rehearsing for *Improvography II* at the Kodak Theatre in Hollywood in March 2005 were (from left) Savion Glover, Maurice Chestnut, Ashley DeForest, and Cartier Williams. Glover would also sing during the show, often songs made famous by Frank Sinatra.

brings our own understanding of tap, our own chapter, to the music." Glover also reintroduced crooning into his show, as he performed songs made famous by Frank Sinatra, like "The Way You Look Tonight" and "One for My Baby, One More for the Road."

Perhaps Glover's most ambitious production to date has been the highly lauded *Classical Savion*, an evening of his feet tappin' to the music of Bach, Beethoven, Vivaldi, and Mendelssohn. In this show, Glover has replaced blues music with that of Bach, and 'da funk Glover is so noted for is being generated by the likes of composer Béla Bartók. Like his other shows, *Classical Savion* had its debut at the Joyce Theater in New York. Only at the end of the show does Glover depart from the classical masters, tappin' his way through one of his signature pieces "The Stars and Stripes Forever (for Now)," based on the John Phillip Sousa marching tune. Of this new concert by Glover, Susan Reiter wrote in *Dance Review Times*:

> Throughout the evening, a framed photo of the late Gregory Hines sat on the piano, looking out at the audience, and Glover momentarily acknowledged it as he left the stage. A mentor and inspiration to his younger colleague, Hines would no doubt have been excited and moved by the bold new challenges Glover has taken on.

CARRYING THE TORCH

At just 32 years of age, Savion Glover has a whole lot of creativity left in him. He also has other responsibilities as a husband to his wife, Nina, and as a father to their son, Chaney, who was born in November 2004. Because he has done so much so young, people often ask Glover if he is afraid he will run out of rhythms and sounds. He says he will not, because the rhythms and sounds are everywhere, all the time.

As he has matured as a man and a performer, Glover has felt a strong responsibility to his craft. He also feels it is his duty to carry on the art form that is tap. Just as Gregory Hines felt the torch had been passed to him to keep tap alive when Sammy Davis, Jr., died, so, too, does Glover feel that Hines's death left him to carry the torch. He appreciates the

IN HIS OWN WORDS...

During an interview with *The New York Times*, Savion Glover said that he wanted to do it all—more acting, more singing, more dancing. When asked if a Las Vegas lounge act was in the future, Glover laughed and said:

> Yeah, why not? I could do the stool and the mike stand with a little ashtray.

compliments people give him about his talent—they tell him that he is the best. But Glover is more in awe of those who came before him—Hines, Chaney, Green, Slyde, Briggs— what they did and can still do in their 50s, 60s, and even 70s. He has a tremendous respect for all of them.

Savion Glover has never done anything besides dance and cannot imagine doing anything else. As he said in the close of his autobiography:

> …[D]ancing is it for me. Just it. There's no person, no food or drink, no movie part going to change my mind about that. I mean, in my mind I'm a tap dancer. How many people can say that? How many people can say what they are? It's one thing to say, 'Okay, I'm a celebrity now, I'm going to get me a TV show.' Nothing wrong with that, understand, but I'm a tap dancer first.

No doubt Savion Glover will keep at his craft. And in that pursuit he will try to bring tap to as many people as he can, perhaps making it as popular someday as baseball, football, or music. He will honor those who came before him, and he will keep teaching what he knows to the up-and-coming tappers of the next generation, so that tap's fiery torch can continue to burn.

1973 Born November 19 in Newark, New Jersey

1978 Enrolls in Suzuki classes at the Newark School of Performing Arts

1980 Joins the band Three Plus

1982 Three Plus plays at the Broadway Dance Center; his mother, Yvette, enrolls Savion in the dance program at the Broadway Dance Center

1984 Auditions for *The Tap Dance Kid* workshop; takes the title role in the show in September; appears in more than 300 performances before the show closes on August 11, 1985

1988 Goes to Paris, France, to perform in *Black and Blue,* tapping with hoofer greats Bunny Briggs, Jimmy Slyde, Lon Chaney, and George Hillman

1989 Appears in *Black and Blue* on Broadway; earns a Tony Award nomination; appears in the film *Tap*

1990 Begins a recurring role on the children's show *Sesame Street*; continues on the program until 1995

1991 Receives the Martin Luther King, Jr., Outstanding Youth Award

1992 Appears in *Jelly's Last Jam* on Broadway; earns a Drama Desk Award nomination; is the youngest recipient of a National Endowment for the Arts grant

1995 Stars in and choreographs *Bring in 'Da Noise, Bring in 'Da Funk,* which opens at the Public Theater on November 15

1996 *Bring in 'Da Noise, Bring in 'Da Funk* transfers to Broadway on April 25; Glover wins Tony and Drama Desk awards for Best Choreography

1997 Forms a dance company called Not Your Ordinary Tappers

1998 Choreographs *The Rat Pack*; stars in *The Wall*; emcees and performs in *Savion Glover's Stomp, Slide and Swing: In Performance at the White House*

1999 Produces *Savion Glover/Downtown: Live Communication*

2000 Goes on tour with *Savion! In Concert: Footnotes*; stars in Spike Lee's film *Bamboozled*

2002 Performs at the Winter Olympics in Salt Lake City, Utah

2003 Friend and mentor Gregory Hines dies on August 9; brings *Improvography* to the stage

2004 Choreographs *Timmy the Great*; son, Chaney, is born in November

2005 Opens new shows *Improvography II* and *Classical Savion*

De Angelis, Gina. *Gregory Hines.* Philadelphia: Chelsea House Publishers, 1999.

Frank, Rusty E. *TAP! The Greatest Tap Dance Stars and Their Stories 1900–1955.* Cambridge, Mass.: Da Capo Press, 1995.

Frommer, Harvey and Myrna Katz Frommer. *It Happened on Broadway: An Oral History of the Great White Way.* Orlando, Fla.: Harcourt Press, 1998.

Glover, Savion and Bruce Weber. *Savion! My Life in Tap.* New York: William Morrow and Company, Inc., 2000.

Gray, Acia. *The Souls of Your Feet: A Tap Dance Guidebook for Rhythm Explorers.* Austin, Tex.: Grand Weaver's Publishing, 1998.

Knowles, Mark. *Tap Roots: The Early History of Tap Dancing.* Jefferson, N.C.: McFarland & Company, 2002.

Valis Hill, Constance and Gregory Hines. *Brotherhood in Rhythm: The Jazz Tap Dancing of the Nicholas Brothers.* New York: Oxford University Press, 2000.

WEBSITES

American Tap Dance Foundation
www.atdf.org

History of Tap Dance
www.offjazz.com/tp-hist.htm

The Public Theater
www.publictheater.org

Tap Dance Homepage
www.tapdance.org

Tony Awards
www.tonyawards.com

page:

Judy L. Hasday, a native of Pennsylvania, received her B.A. in communications and her M.Ed. in instructional technologies from Temple University. A certified Ophthalmic Assistant, Ms. Hasday has written many articles in the field of ophthalmology, as well as dozens of books for young adults. These include the New York Public Library "Books for the Teen Age" award winners *James Earl Jones* (1999) and *The Holocaust* (2003), and the National Social Studies Council "2001 Notable Social Studies Trade Book for Young People" award winner, *Extraordinary Women Athletes*. Her free time is devoted to photography, travel, and her pets: cat Sassy and four zebra finches, Scotch, B.J., Atticus, and Jacob.